Praise for *Change Your Brain, Change Your Grades*

"Working with college students every day, I am keenly aware of the difference that the principles and practices of *Change Your Brain, Change Your Grades* can have on student success. This is a must-read for parents, educators, and students who are longing to thrive and excel."
—**Michael J. Beals, PhD, president of Vanguard University**

"Your mind is all. Everything you will ever be, become, do or have is processed through your mind-brain connection. My friend, Dr. Daniel Amen, knows more about helping you change your brain, so you can expand, improve, and accelerate your progress and become all you were meant to be. Enjoy reading his insightful brilliance and wisdom, so you can fulfill yourself, conquer all your challenges, and make a difference that makes a difference. You are worth it—read this and prosper mightily."
—**Mark Victor Hansen, cocreator of the**
Chicken Soup for the Soul series

"With a daughter entering grad school, this volume in the Change Your Brain series could not have been more timely. With the *Change Your Brain, Change Grades* resource, her brain will be at its optimal performance."
—**Jack Felton, marriage and family therapist**
at New Hope Counseling Center

"This is an extraordinary book and a must-read for all students from elementary school through college, including parents. I loved every single chapter. A class that teaches this material would be appropriate at all educational levels and would certainly increase academic grades. There is a flow to the writing and information presented that is understandable and easy to remember. Daniel Amen's book will positively enhance the lives of students everywhere."
—**Colonel (R) Jill W. Chambers, US Army**

"*Change Your Brain, Change Your Grades* will change your life. Dr. Daniel Amen provides the tools students of all ages need to succeed with better results and less stress. A great read, scientifically solid, and packed full of practical advice that will make a difference for anyone who wants to be better at learning how to learn."

—**W. Lee Warren, MD, author of** *I've Seen the End of You: A Neurosurgeon's Look at Faith, Doubt, and the Things We Think We Know*

"The information in this book is making a meaningful difference in the lives of countless people—including my own family! Because of Dr. Amen's ground-breaking work, my son went from struggling with focus to flourishing in school. In my positive psychology programs with schools and corporations, I see many applications for Daniel's evidence-based tools!"

—**Fatima Doman, author of** *Authentic Strengths* **and** *True You: Authentic Strengths for Kids;* **creator of** *Authentic Strengths Resilience for Students*

"Dr. Amen's book *Change Your Brain, Change Your Life* spent over 40 weeks on the *New York Times* bestseller list, because it struck a chord with millions of readers and now a new book has emerged: *Change Your Brain, Change Your Grades.* This seminal and timely work is a must-read for all students at any educational level, especially in our competitive world. Direct and a delight to read, it will help smooth the road into a bright and successful future to all readers."

—**Andrew Campbell, MD, editor in chief of** *Alternative Therapies in Health and Medicine* **and** *Advances in Mind-Body Medicine*

"*Change Your Brain, Change Your Grades* is an engaging and easy to read book translating neuroscience into personalized strategies to optimize learning. It is a must read for those who want to get the most from education and take control of their lives. It is certain to become another bestseller by Dr. Amen."

—**Ed Pigott, PhD, research psychologist and associate editor of** *NeuroRegulation*

"I wish I had known all that Dr. Amen discusses in this book when I was a teenager. *Change Your Brain, Change Your Grades* contains incredible material for students in high school or higher education. Dr. Amen says, 'You can change your learning strategies and thereby change your success,' and so your classes become more enjoyable and productive by studying smarter, not harder! Dr. Amen captures your attention with his use of mnemonics and practical references, even to Biblical illustrations. Tech tips by Chloe and Alizé are a brilliant addition! You are left with a goldmine of tips and resources for study. Dr. Amen convinced me that learning never stops. Age is not debilitating but rather good brain health, at any age, is a positive factor that leads us to the choices we make, and the choices we make reveal the successes we have—even in the senior years of life."

—Rosemary Wright Jackson, former alumni director
and former assistant to the president for alumni affairs
at Vanguard University of Southern California

"A very high percentage of our patients struggle with ADD/ADHD. Their history in school has always been a frustrating one. They are told things like, 'You're not performing up to your intelligence or abilities.' It has led to great shame and discouragement. We've been working with Dr. Amen and his integrative treatment plans for over 20 years and have seen great success for our patients and their relationships. This book offers very practical help for ADD/ADHD and is another helpful contribution from Dr. Amen to help people live well."

—Mark Laaser, PhD, MDiv and Debbie Laaser,
MA, LMFT, coauthors of *Seven Desires*

"Graduation is like summiting Everest. Both demand preparation, discipline and strategies devised. All well-practiced before heading out of basecamp or, into a pre-exam night. For students, *Change Your Brain, Change Your Grades* breaks ominous mountains into manageable terrain with skills expanding their capacity to learn . . . all the way to the summit."

—Karen Lansing, MFT, BCETS

"This book is a powerful guide to help you improve your studying habits and optimize your grades, as well as your brain in the process. Thoughtfully and clearly explained from the heart by brain imaging expert Dr. Amen, it offers great tips and tricks, and is a must have for anyone wishing to take their academic performance to the next level. I wish I had such a study guide when I was a student, as it would have helped me avoid some of the costly mistakes made when studying as an undergraduate and beyond!"

—Ruth Mary Allan, PhD, certified high performance
coach and business performance consultant

"*Change Your Brain, Change Your Grades* adds the missing piece for students who want to get better grades—THEIR BRAIN. Your brain is the most powerful organ in human history. Get it right and you will thrive."

—Jim Kwik, memory expert and CEO of Kwik Learning

"I have had the privilege and honor of working with Dr. Amen for over 25 years. Recently, a young man graduated from a major university in Southern California on the honor roll. He finished his bachelor's degree in two years after having spent the previous four years struggling to finish a community college. Years of struggle and failure from elementary school on. One look at his brain, and it was clear the supplements and medications he needed. He went from failure to success and is now headed for a great career in business. It all started with a look at the brain. In *Change Your Brain Change Your Grades*, you will find the answers you have been looking for . . . for yourself, your children and possibly grandchildren. Give a gift of academic success . . . buy this book and give it to someone you know who is struggling, help them get a scan, and discover the road to success!"

—Dr. Earl R. Henslin, clinical psychologist and
author of *This Is Your Brain on Joy*

"Every student has something to learn from this book. Success in life is sometimes about working harder and sometimes about working smarter. In addition to sharing his own personal stories of learning to work smarter, Dr. Amen presents multiple strategies for identifying your brain type and improving your brain's function so your efforts will be rewarded."

—Michelle Flowers, MD, child and adolescent psychiatrist

Praise for *Change Your Brain, Change Your Life*

"*Change Your Brain, Change Your Life* is your manual for fully optimizing your brain. Dr. Amen and I partner with Pastor Rick Warren in creating The Daniel Plan that has helped tens of thousands of people get well by using habits that optimize decision making and brain function. His newly revised book gives readers a powerfully practical exploration into the organ that makes you who you are."

—Mark Hyman, MD, Director of the Cleveland Center for Functional Medicine and author of the #1 *New York Times* bestseller *The Blood Sugar Solution*.

"After 110,000 brain scans Dr. Daniel Amen is *the ultimate expert* on how to change your brain so that you can change your life for the better. The discovery of his wisdom and insights will make your life and brain health infinitely better."

—Mark Victor Hansen, *New York Times* bestselling author and co-creator of the *Chicken Soup for the Soul* series and *The Miracles In You* series

Praise for *Healing ADD*

"REVOLUTIONARY . . . I strongly urge anyone with a family member who suffers with ADD to read this book."

—Barry Sears, author of *The Zone*

"For parents of children with ADD, adults with ADD, therapists, and physicians. The subtypes Dr. Amen has firmly established will help clinicians everywhere tailor ADD treatments to each and every individual. One size does not fit all."

—George Delgado, MD, FAAFP, associate clinical professor, University of California, Davis

Praise for *Memory Rescue*

"Dr. Amen helped to rescue my memory and brain, which changed my life. *Memory Rescue* will give you strategies to quickly improve your memory and brain now and for the rest of your life. I highly recommend it."

—Dave Asprey, founder and CEO of Bulletproof 360

"*Memory Rescue* is a powerful new book that shows you step-by-step how to improve your memory and overall health. The information is smart, simple, research-based, and effective. It's your roadmap to the best brain possible."

—Mark Hyman, MD, physician and best-selling author

"This is an incredibly helpful book for anyone who wants to increase their brain capacity and strengthen their memory. I want to stay sharp, and that's why I read everything Dr. Amen writes, and you should too!"

—Pastor Rick Warren, author of *The Purpose Driven Life* and *The Daniel Plan*

Praise for *Feel Better Fast*

"Daniel has taught me (and countless others) the critical role our brain health plays in our careers, families, and overall quality of life. If you truly value the relationships in your life, stop what you're doing and read this book."

—Todd Davis, Franklin Covey's chief people officer; *Wall Street Journal* bestselling author of *Get Better*

"Our choices determine our results, and our results determine our success. It all begins with choices. But the question is, which choices are right? How can we choose to live with joy, creativity, and prosperity, and free ourselves from depression and panic? With his astonishing new research, Daniel Amen has unlocked the answers. In this book, you'll discover new aspects of who you are and who you can become. Once you understand your own emotions and behaviors, you can replace the negative with a positive future. This book outlines the game plan to your most fascinating and fulfilling life."

  —Sally Hogshead, *New York Times* **bestselling author and**
   creator of the Fascination Advantage personality test

CHANGE YOUR
BRAIN
CHANGE YOUR
GRADES

Also by Daniel Amen

Feel Better Fast and Make It Last, Tyndale, 2018

Memory Rescue, Tyndale, 2017

Stones of Remembrance, with Stephen Arterburn, Tyndale, 2017

Captain Snout and the Superpower Questions, Zonderkidz 2017

The Brain Warrior's Way, with Tana Amen,
New American Library, 2016

The Brain Warrior's Way Cookbook, with Tana
Amen, New American Library, 2016

Time for Bed, Sleepyhead, Zonderkidz, 2016

Change Your Brain, Change Your Life, Three Rivers
Press, 2015 (Revised), *NY Times* Bestseller

Healing ADD, Putnam, 2013 (revised), *NY Times* Bestseller

The Daniel Plan, with Rick Warren and Mark Hyman,
MD, Zondervan, 2013, #1 *NY Times* Bestseller

Unleash the Power of the Female Brain, Harmony Books, 2013

Use Your Brain to Change Your Age, Crown Archetype, 2012,
NY Times Bestseller

The Amen Solution, Crown Archetype 2011, *NY Times* Bestseller

Unchain Your Brain, MindWorks, 2010

Change Your Brain, Change Your Body, Harmony
Books, 2010, *NY Times* Bestseller

Magnificent Mind at Any Age, Harmony
Books, 2009, *NY Times* Bestseller

The Brain in Love, Three Rivers Press, 2007

Making a Good Brain Great, Harmony Books,
2005, Amazon Book of the Year

Preventing Alzheimer's, with William R. Shankle, MD, Putnam, 2004

Healing Anxiety and Depression, with Lisa
Routh, MD, Putnam, 2003

New Skills for Frazzled Parents, MindWorks, 2003

Healing the Hardware of the Soul, Free Press, 2002

ADD in Intimate Relationships, MindWorks, 1997

*The Most Important Thing in Life I Learned
from a Penguin*, MindWorks, 1994

CHANGE YOUR
BRAIN
CHANGE YOUR
GRADES

The Secrets of Successful Students:
Science-Based Strategies to Boost Memory,
Strengthen Focus, and Study Faster

DANIEL G. AMEN, MD

with Chloe Amen and Alizé Castellanos

BenBella Books, Inc.
Dallas, TX

Copyright © 2019 by Daniel G. Amen

BenBella Books, Inc.
10440 N. Central Expressway, Suite 800
Dallas, TX 75231
www.benbellabooks.com
Send feedback to feedback@benbellabooks.com

Printed in the United States of America
10 9 8 7 6 5 4 3 2 1

Library of Congress Cataloging-in-Publication Data is available upon request.
9781948836852 (trade paper)
9781948836869 (electronic)

Proofreading by Jenny Bridges and Lisa Story
Text design and composition by Aaron Edmiston
Cover design by Ty Nowicki
Printed by Lake Book Manufacturing

Distributed to the trade by Two Rivers Distribution, an Ingram brand
www.tworiversdistribution.com

*To all of the students, young and old, that have
come through Amen Clinics over the years.
I will always root for your success.*

CONTENTS

CHANGE YOUR BRAIN, CHANGE YOUR GRADES IS DIRECTED AT YOU

POP QUIZ: WHAT KIND OF STUDENT ARE YOU?

1. Do you feel like you should be getting better grades?
2. Does schoolwork stress you out?
3. When you need to study, does it take longer than you'd like because everything is so disorganized?
4. Are you spending more time studying than the A students in your class but not getting the same results?
5. Do you study so much you miss out on other things you'd like to do?
6. Are you heading back to school after a long break and need a refresher to get more done in less time?
7. Do you feel like you're failing in your academic life?
8. Would you love some simple, practical tips to make studying easier, to feel more confident in your abilities, and to actually start to enjoy the learning process?

If you answered yes to any of these questions, this book is for you.

All of the great writers about success—think Ben Franklin, Dale Carnegie, Stephen Covey, and Sheryl Sandberg—have overlooked the most important secret of success, because they did not have the technology to see it. Based on the world's largest brain imaging database, we now know that success and failure everywhere in life starts, and is maintained, between your ears, in the moment-by-moment functioning of your brain.

Your brain is involved in everything you do and everything you are, including how you think, feel, act, and interact with others. Your brain is the organ of love, learning, personality, character, and every decision you make. After looking at more than 150,000 brain scans over the last 30 years, I have learned that when your brain works right, you work right—whether we're talking about school, work, relationships, money, health, or anything else. Likewise, when your brain is troubled for whatever reason, you are much more likely to have trouble in your life. Get your brain right and learning will be much easier for you.

I will admit that I was merely an average student in middle school and high school, but I went on to graduate near the top of my class in college and medical school. How did I do it? I used my brain to develop simple strategies that allowed me to study and learn more efficiently. If I can do it, you can, too.

Change Your Brain, Change Your Grades draws on my experience as a neuroscientist and psychiatrist, as well as the latest brain science, to help you study more effectively, learn faster, and stay focused so you can achieve your academic goals. It is also based on a brain health program I created with Dr. Jesse Payne that teaches students how to love and care for their brains. Called Brain Thrive by 25 (www.brainthriveby25.com), it has been taught in all 50 states and seven countries. In the course, we include lessons on basic brain facts, the developing brain, gender differences, the impact of drugs and alcohol on the brain, nutrition, stress management, killing ANTs (automatic negative thoughts), and how to throw a brain healthy party. A popular course, it has changed the lives of those who take it.

Many of the regions of the brain are involved in determining if a student will be successful or be stuck struggling to graduate. In chapter 1, you will learn about some of the brain regions and the role each plays in helping you learn and retain information, stay organized, pay attention in class, and feel confident in your abilities. Every brain is unique, and understanding your brain type (more on this in chapter 2) and how your unique brain works is an important step. By using the simple strategies in this book, you can optimize your brain so you can become a more successful student, no matter what your age.

> If you suspect you might have learning issues or ADD/ADHD, take the Amen Clinics Learning Disability Questionnaire in Appendix B and seek treatment if necessary.

This book can help a broad range of students, whether you're an underachiever, a stressed-out studier, an adult reentering school or doing job-related training, or just someone who wants to make learning easier.

Underachievers. If your achievements fall below your capabilities, you may think you're a mediocre student because of so-so intelligence or because you don't have a high IQ. But did you know that research shows that learning strategies are actually more important than IQ when predicting academic achievement?[1] In truth your knowledge of *how* to learn effectively and efficiently may be mediocre but not your *ability* to learn. The good news is you can change your learning strategies and thereby change your success. Think how great it would feel if you had the upper hand in a classroom full of other students. Wouldn't it make learning so much more fun and enjoyable? I have seen C students become consistent B and even A students after acquiring these skills, and with much less stress.

Stressed-out studiers. This book is also useful for good students who feel like they need to use massive assault tactics when they study in order to achieve. Do you neglect other areas of your life in the race to reach scholastic success? You may think that that in order to be an A+ student, your nose should be buried in a textbook until 2 a.m. every day, but that is not realistic or even healthy. How would you like to learn to direct your efforts and economize your time so you can achieve the same results in less time with less stress, leaving room for personal development, more fun, and a more balanced life?

Adults reentering school or doing job-related training. *Change Your Brain, Change Your Grades* is also for the working person who is either going back to school after a long absence or is taking on job-related training. It has been estimated that almost one-quarter of the adult population in the United States is enrolled in some form of regular study, and that people in skilled professions or trades require retraining every five to six years to keep up to date with new developments in their fields. If you're one of these people, you probably have more outside responsibilities than the typical college student and have less time to devote to your studies. This means you need to use the most efficient study methods possible in order to accomplish your goals. Finding tricks and so-called shortcuts is *not* taking the easy way out; it's going the extra mile to achieve the success you want while making your life happier and less stressful.

Anyone who wants to make learning easier. Whether you want to learn a foreign language before taking a vacation, take a finance course so you can increase your investing know-how, or simply ace your tests with less effort, you can benefit from the strategies in this book. The principles in this book are practical and can easily be applied to almost any learning situation.

SIX WAYS *CHANGE YOUR BRAIN, CHANGE YOUR GRADES* IS DIFFERENT

Many books have been written on how to study. What makes this one different? *Change Your Brain, Change Your Grades* will systematically look at each major area of what I call "studenthood" and offer many practical solutions. This book will also give you the necessary mental boost you need to not only thrive, but to actually enjoy the learning process.

Here are six ways this book is unique:

1. It teaches you how to optimize the organ of learning—your brain.
2. Much more than just a book on how to study, this is a handbook on how to benefit from being a student, how to profit personally by excelling as a student, and how to do both of these without jeopardizing other areas of your life.

3. This book was written by someone who studies human brains and behavior for a living. As a psychiatrist, neuroscientist, and brain health expert, I have worked with thousands of students of all ages who are struggling in school and who have improved their success with the same strategies in this book. It's been a while since I've been in school, so I also asked my teenage daughter, Chloe, and niece, Alizé, to help make this book relevant for 21st-century students. Look for the "Tech Tip from Chloe and Alizé" boxes throughout this book for their insights on how to use technology in the most effective way.

4. The secrets to learning involve so much more than just test prep, time management, and organization skills. This book will introduce you to the power of changing your habits and finding your motivation (chapter 3), preparation (chapter 4), class skills (chapter 8), studying with a partner (chapter 10), and approaching teachers (chapter 11.)

5. Every method or suggestion outlined in this book has been tested and proven with thousands of students. I am not going to tell you what other people think. I am going to tell you what I know works!

6. This book is not meant to be an exhaustive textbook on how to excel in all subjects. Think of it as your go-to guidebook—providing inspiration, practical ideas, and a pleasant sense of relief from the everyday academic grind. You can read it quickly and reap its benefits immediately. And when you master the skills in this book, you can learn any subject faster and retain the information longer.

WORK SMARTER, NOT HARDER

With the tools and strategies in this book, you'll discover how to work smarter, not harder. You'll stop wasting time on aimless study and focus on the most important things, so you can learn more with less effort. You'll develop skills that will serve you well during school and throughout your life as you continue to learn. Of course, as you master these skills, your grades, confidence, and even your social life will reap the benefits. In particular, this book will help you:

1. Kick bad study habits to the curb and adopt smarter study habits.
2. Discover how to prepare better for classes, so you get more out of them with less overall study time.
3. Adopt a big-picture view that helps you develop a solid foundation for learning anything faster.
4. Organize yourself and your time more efficiently.
5. Understand the different study methods and learn to choose the ones best suited to you.
6. Learn to zero in on the most important points in lectures and take better notes.
7. Memorize faster and remember it longer.
8. Learn how to pick a study partner and discover why two brains are sometimes better than one.
9. Approach and communicate with teachers so they become a valuable resource for you instead of viewing them as critics of your work.
10. Skillfully prepare for and perform better on exams.
11. Improve your writing and speaking skills.
12. Discover how to boost your confidence by killing the ANTs (automatic negative thoughts) that threaten your success.
13. Get the best out of yourself.

GET ON THE BUS!

In his book *The Great Divorce*, C. S. Lewis writes about a group of people in Hell. Lewis makes it clear that the people, through their actions and attitudes, are responsible for their disadvantageous situation. The people are offered a chance to take an intense bus ride from Hell toward Heaven. Only after choosing to get on the bus and ride on the path toward change can they avail themselves of the opportunity to improve their circumstances. By choosing *Change Your Brain, Change Your Grades,* you have obtained your bus ticket for a more satisfying "studenthood." Now, get on the bus and ride on toward efficient methods of study and better grades—making sure you enjoy yourself along the way!

1

OPTIMIZE YOUR BRAIN

THE FIRST STEP TO MORE SUCCESS IN SCHOOL

The human brain is the most complex and wondrous organ in the universe. Your ability to succeed in school comes from many different areas of your brain. If you want to perform better in the classroom, you must first learn about your brain. After all, it is your brain that decides if you should play mindless video games or head to the library to study. It is your brain that tells you to ditch class or pay close attention to the professor's lecture. It is your brain that causes you to procrastinate and have to pull an all-nighter or that helps you plan ahead so you can get a good night's sleep before a big test. In this chapter we will look at different systems within the brain, what they do, and the strengths and vulnerabilities they give us. We will also explore three strategies to optimize your brain, which is the first step to becoming a more successful student. But first, here are 41 amazing facts about your brain:

1. The brain has about 100 billion neurons (brain cells).
2. Each neuron is connected to other neurons by up to 10,000 connections.
3. The brain has more connections than there are stars in the universe.
4. A piece of brain tissue the size of a grain of sand contains 100,000 neurons and over a billion connections talking to one another.
5. The brain prunes connections it does not use: Use it or lose it.

6. The brain weighs about 3 pounds, or roughly 2 percent of your body's weight.

7. Yet, it uses 20 to 30 percent of the calories you consume;

8. 20 percent of the oxygen you breathe; and

9. 20 percent of the blood flow in your body.

10. The brain needs a constant supply of oxygen. As little as five minutes without oxygen can cause some brain cells to die, leading to severe brain damage.

11. It is the consistency of soft butter, tofu, or custard.

12. It is easily damaged.

13. Your soft brain is housed in a very hard skull that has many sharp, bony ridges.

14. Your brain has the storage capacity of 6 million years' worth of *The Wall Street Journal*.

15. It is about 80 percent water.

16. Being dehydrated by just 2 percent can negatively affect attention, memory, and judgment.

17. About 60 percent of the dry weight of the brain is fat.

18. Low-fat diets are generally bad for the brain.

19. About 25 percent of the body's cholesterol is in the brain and is essential for brain health.

20. Total cholesterol levels under 160 have been associated with homicide, suicide, depression, and death from all causes.

21. Babies have big heads in order to hold their rapidly growing brains.

22. A 2-year-old's brain is 80 percent the size of an adult's brain.

23. The brain peaks in activity around age 8, then declines until it is settled at about age 25, which, by the way, is when car insurance rates change, because people make better decisions on the road and most everywhere else in their lives when their brains are fully developed.

24. Brain information travels up to 268 miles per hour, faster than Formula 1 race cars (about 240 mph).

25. The brain constantly generates 12 to 25 watts of electricity.

26. The average brain generates up to 50,000 thoughts per day.

27. The brain processes a visual image in as little as 13 milliseconds, which is less than a blink of an eye.

28. One of the world's most powerful computers (Japan's K computer) was programmed to simulate human brain activity; it took 40 minutes to process the information equal to 1 second of brain activity.

29. When you stop learning, the brain starts dying.

30. Inflammation is a major cause of depression and dementia.

31. Gum disease increases brain inflammation.

32. Fish consumption helps decrease brain inflammation.

33. Depression doubles the risk of Alzheimer's disease in women and quadruples it in men.

34. The brain cleans or washes itself at night, which is why getting at least 7 hours (or 8 to 10 hours if you're a teen) of sleep is important.

35. Soldiers who got 7 hours of sleep at night shot with 98 percent accuracy at the firing range the next day; those who got just 6 hours were only 50 percent accurate; 5 hours were 35 percent accurate; and 4 hours only 15 percent accurate (they were dangerous).

36. Gut health is critical to brain health. Your gut makes vitamins and neurotransmitters essential to brain health.

37. Alcohol prevents the formation of new memories.

38. Alcohol is not a health food for the brain.

39. In research my team published, marijuana prematurely aged the brain.

40. About 30 percent of the brain is dedicated to vision, which explains why we are more drawn to images than to text.

41. Children exposed to violence show the same brain activity as soldiers exposed to war.

A BRIEF TOUR OF YOUR BRAIN

The most noticeable structure in the brain is the cerebral cortex, the wrinkly mass that sits atop and covers the rest of the brain. The cortex has four main areas, called lobes, on each side of the brain, and another important structure called the cerebellum.

1. Frontal lobes (specifically, the prefrontal cortex, or PFC): purposeful movement, planning, and forethought
2. Temporal lobes: visual and auditory processing, memory, learning, mood stability
3. Parietal lobes: direction sense, math, constructing
4. Occipital lobes: process visual images
5. Cerebellum: motor skills, thought coordination, processing complex information

**When your brain works right, you work well in school.
When your brain is troubled, you have trouble in school.**

When your brain is healthy, you tend to be effective, creative, attentive, and organized. When your brain is troubled—for whatever reason—you are much more likely to have problems at school, including issues with planning, focus, organization, and memory. Even subtle brain issues can get in the way of achieving your academic goals. The great news is that you are not stuck with the brain you have. You can change your brain and change your grades. Optimizing your brain is the first step to becoming a more successful student.

To optimize your brain, you need to follow three simple strategies.

- Love your brain.
- Avoid the things that hurt your brain.
- Do the things that help your brain.

YOUR BRAIN: A BRIEF PRIMER

Outside View of the Brain

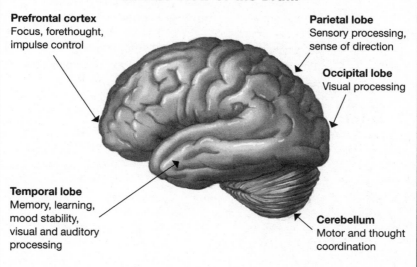

Prefrontal cortex
Focus, forethought,
impulse control

Parietal lobe
Sensory processing,
sense of direction

Occipital lobe
Visual processing

Temporal lobe
Memory, learning,
mood stability,
visual and auditory
processing

Cerebellum
Motor and thought
coordination

Inside View of the Brain

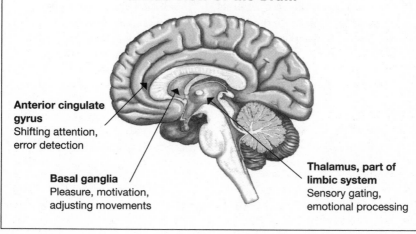

**Anterior cingulate
gyrus**
Shifting attention,
error detection

Basal ganglia
Pleasure, motivation,
adjusting movements

**Thalamus, part of
limbic system**
Sensory gating,
emotional processing

Brain Regions: Functions and Problems

Brain System	Functions	Problems
Prefrontal Cortex	Focus Forethought Planning Judgment Impulse control Organization Empathy Learning from experience	Short attention span Distractibility Lack of perseverance Impulse control problems Restlessness Chronic lateness Poor time management Disorganization Procrastination Unavailability of emotions Poor judgment Trouble learning from experience Lower empathy
Anterior Cingulate Gyrus	Ability to shift attention Cognitive flexibility Adaptability Movement from idea to idea Ability to see options Ability to "go with the flow" Ability to cooperate Ability to detect errors or when things are not right	Strong will Worrying Holding on to hurts from the past Getting stuck on thoughts (obsessions) Getting stuck on behaviors (compulsions) Oppositional behavior Argumentativeness Uncooperativeness Tendency to say no automatically Addictive behaviors (alcohol or drug abuse, eating disorders) Cognitive inflexibility Chronic pain Obsessive-compulsive disorder (OCD)

Basal Ganglia	Integrating feeling and movement Forming habits Controlling motivation and drive Setting the body's anxiety level Shifting and steadying fine motor movements Suppressing unwanted motor behaviors Mediating pleasure and ecstasy	Anxiety or nervousness Physical sensations of anxiety Tendency to predict the worst Conflict avoidance Risk avoidance Tourette's syndrome (tics) Muscle tension, soreness Tremors Fine motor problems Low or excessive motivation Sensitivity to rejection Social anxiety, interpersonal inhibition
Thalamus/ Limbic System	Sets the emotional tone of the mind Filters external events through internal states Tags events as internally important Stores highly charged emotional memories Modulates motivation Controls appetite and sleep cycles Promotes bonding Directly processes the sense of smell Modulates libido	Sadness or clinical depression Increased negative thinking Negative perception of events Flood of negative emotions, such as hopelessness, helplessness, and guilt Appetite and sleep problems Decreased or increased sexual responsiveness Social isolation Pain

Temporal Lobes	Hearing/listening Reading Reading social cues, including speech and tone Short-term memory Long-term memory Recognizing objects by sight Mood stability Naming things	Mishearing communication Dyslexia Socially inappropriate behavior Trouble reading social cues Memory problems Word-finding problems Poor visual recognition Mood instability Abnormal sensory perceptions Anger, irritability, dark thoughts
Parietal Lobes	Direction sense Sensory perception Spatial processing Seeing movement Visual guidance, such as to grab objects Recognizing objects by touch Ability to know where you are in space Knowing right from left Reading and creating maps	Trouble with math or writing Impaired direction sense Trouble dressing or putting objects together Left/right confusion Denial of illness Impaired position sense Neglect or unawareness of what you see Impaired copying, drawing, or cutting
Occipital Lobes	Sight Color perception Lines Depth perception	Deficits in vision Deficits in perception Visual hallucination Visual illusions Functional blindness
Cerebellum	Thought coordination Speed of thought (like clock speed of a computer) Organization Motor coordination Impulse control	Poor learning Slowed thinking Disorganization Impulsiveness Coordination problems Slowed walking Slowed speech

Love your brain. Most students never think about their brain as a tool for learning. You (or your parents) will buy all sorts of gadgets to help you in your studies, but it's your brain that is worthy of your biggest investment. Loving your brain means always keeping it in mind when you make choices. Whenever you are making a decision, ask yourself, "Is this decision good for my brain or bad for my brain?"

Avoid the things that hurt your brain. There are many things in our everyday lives that can hurt your brain and make it harder for you to do well in school:

- Lack of exercise
- Negative thoughts
- Chronic stress
- Head trauma
- Environmental toxins
- Drugs
- Excessive alcohol
- Mental health issues
- Many medications
- Hormonal imbalances
- Junk food diet
- Obesity
- Lack of sleep

Do the things that help your brain. What's exciting is that there are many things that can boost your brain power and help optimize brain function:

- Learning new things
- Having loving relationships
- Having a purpose in life
- Physical exercise, especially coordination exercises (table tennis, dancing, etc.)
- Controlling your thinking
- Meditation and stress-relief techniques

- Protecting your head from injury
- Avoiding drugs and too much alcohol
- Getting help for mental health issues
- Balancing hormones
- Great nutrition
- Taking nutrients (omega-3 fatty acids; vitamins B_6, B_{12}, D, and folate)

When you start optimizing your brain, you will find that all the additional tips and tools in this book will become much easier to implement. And this will put you on the fast track to successful studenthood.

2

KNOW YOUR BRAIN TYPE

EVEN IF YOU NEVER GET SCANNED

Why do you act the way you act?
Why do you think the way you think?
How can you perform your best?
How can you interact better with your teachers and other students?

I f you want to know the answers to these profound questions, you must learn about your brain, which governs how you think, feel, act, and interact. Learning about your brain, especially your brain type, will help you in school and can also help you in other areas of your life. And learning about the brain types of others will help improve your relationships with your teachers and fellow students so you can be more successful at school.

In the late 1980s, when I started looking at the brain as a psychiatrist, I was searching for tools to help me be more effective in helping my patients get better faster. My colleagues and I started looking at the brain with a test called quantitative EEG (qEEG), which evaluates the brain's electrical activity. Once we knew an individual's brain pattern, we could then teach the patient to change it, using techniques such as neurofeedback. This is where I first got the inspiration for my book *Change Your Brain, Change Your Life.* We proved that you are not stuck with the brain you have; you can make it better. In 1991, we added brain SPECT (single photon emission computed tomography) imaging to our toolbox.

PRIMING YOUR BRAIN FOR BETTER LEARNING

The preparation for learning begins before you ever crack open a book or set foot inside a classroom. It starts with your brain. If your brain is healthy, it will be much easier for you to learn. If your brain is unhealthy, it will be harder for you to be successful in your studies. Over the past three decades at Amen Clinics, we have taken a revolutionary approach to diagnosing and treating our patients. As part of a comprehensive assessment, we use a brain imaging study called SPECT that looks at blood flow and activity in the brain. In these brain scans, full, symmetrical activity is an indicator of a healthy brain, whereas holes show areas that are significantly low in blood flow and/or activity. *You don't want holes in your brain!* When our patients see their brain, it helps them understand that their issues are not a personal failure but rather a medical issue. It inspires them to develop brain envy and to take the steps necessary to have a healthier brain.

Surface SPECT Scans

Healthy Brain
(looking from the top down)

Toxicity from
Drug and Alcohol Abuse

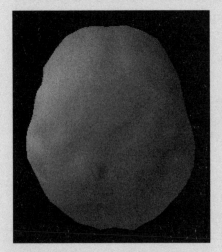 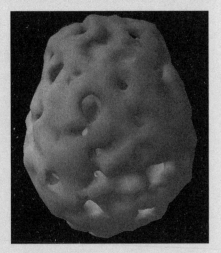

Full, even, symmetrical activity   Scalloping or overall low activity

15-Year-Old Patient with Traumatic Brain Injury

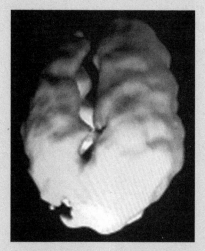

Damage to left hemisphere

Attention Deficit Disorder: Underside Surface Views

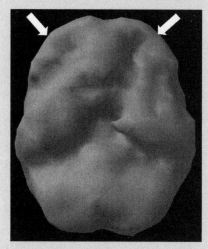

At rest: Good prefrontal
activity (arrows)

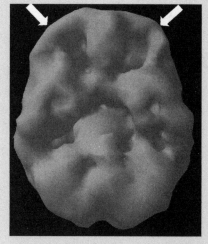

During concentration: Drop-off
of prefrontal activity (arrows)

Teenager with ADD: Underside View

Before treatment   **After treatment**

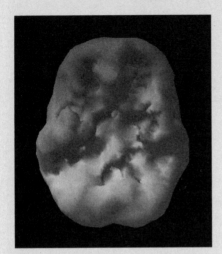 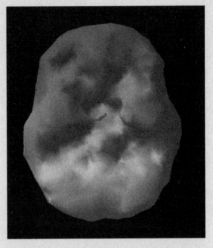

Low frontal lobe activity   Marked overall improvement

Active SPECT Scans

Here are examples of "active" SPECT scans. The gray background represents average activity. The white areas represent the top 15 percent of brain activity, which in adults is mostly in the back, bottom part of the brain, in an area called the cerebellum (Latin for "little brain"). Some 50 percent of the brain's neurons reside in this area.

Healthy Active Scan
(looking from top down)

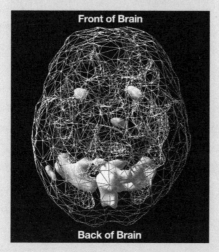

Gray is average activity; white is top 15% showing
most active areas of the brain.

Obsessive Compulsive Traits

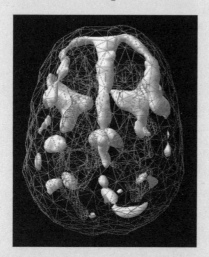

Marked increased activity in frontal lobes.
Frontal lobes work too hard, so they need to be
calmed to help people feel better.

Posttraumatic Stress Disorder

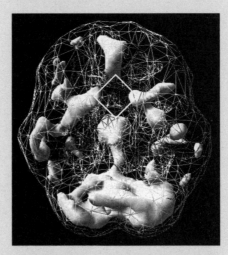

Diamond pattern of increased activity in
deep emotional part of brain (diamond).
Overactive areas need to be calmed.

Even if you don't have a mental health issue, improving your brain health will make it easier to ace your classes without giving up other areas of your life that are important to you. Getting your brain primed for learning is the key. (See chapter 15 for more details and Appendix A for 107 Ways to Grow Your Brain.)

A full-color version of the following poster hangs in over 100,000 schools, prisons, and therapists' offices around the world.

WHICH BRAIN
DO YOU WANT?

HEALTHY
TOP DOWN

HEALTHY
UNDERSIDE

3 YEARS OF
METH

4 YEARS OF
MARIJUANA

ALL AGES · ALL AGES

AGE 28 · AGE 17

DRUGS
DAMAGE
THE BRAIN

AGE 45 · AGE 22

AGE 32 · AGE 38

10 YEARS OF
ALCOHOL

4 YEARS OF
SMOKING

4 YEARS OF
COCAINE

6 YEARS OF
OPIATES

These are brain SPECT (single photon emission computed tomography) images
that assess blood flow and activity. Holes show areas significantly low in activity.

You can make your brain healthy again. Visit www.amenclinics.com to learn how.

Initially, my team started by naively looking for unique electrical or blood flow signature patterns for each of the major mental illnesses—such as anxiety disorders, depression, addictions, bipolar disorder, obsessive compulsive disorder, autism, and ADD/ADHD—but we soon discovered there was not one brain pattern associated with any of these illnesses. Rather, they all have multiple types that require their own treatments. This makes sense because there can never be just one pattern for, say, depression, since not all depressed people are the same. Some are withdrawn, others are angry, and still others are anxious or obsessive. Taking a one-size-fits-all approach to people with mental health issues based on symptom clusters invites failure and frustration.

But the scans did help us understand the type of anxiety, depression, ADHD, obesity, or addiction each person had, so we could better target treatment to that individual's brain. **This one idea led to a dramatic breakthrough in our effectiveness with patients** and opened up a new world of understanding and hope for the tens of thousands of people who have come to see us and the millions of people who have read my books or seen our public television shows. In previously published books, I have written about:

- 7 types of ADD/ADHD
- 7 types of anxiety and depression
- 6 types of addictions
- 5 types of overeaters

Understanding your type of brain is critical to getting the right help.

In addition to looking at mental health problems, we also realized that we were seeing personality types in the scans. The scans revealed so much about people's personalities—including their thinking patterns, behaviors, and interactions with others:

- If the brain's blood flow was full, even, and symmetrical in all areas, we called it **balanced**.

- When areas in the front of the brain were lower in activity or "sleepier" than average, people tended to be impulsive and **spontaneous**.
- When the front areas of the brain were much more active than average, people were more likely to worry more and to be more **persistent**.
- When there was above-average activity in the limbic "emotional" brain, people likely had a greater vulnerability to sadness and tended to be more **sensitive.**
- When activity was higher than average in the basal ganglia and amygdala, people tended to feel more anxious and to be more **cautious**.

In those early years when I performed brain scans, I would often do a "blind" reading, without any information on the patient. With nothing but the scan, I realized I could learn a lot about a person. Of course, with every new patient we evaluate, we take a comprehensive look at their lives. Still, I had a lot of fun asking people, "Would you say you have a tendency to think this way . . .?" based solely on their scans.

We once saw a teacher who wanted to learn more about our process in helping students with learning issues and ADHD so she could feel more comfortable recommending our services to parents who were looking for help for their children. She wanted to have her brain scanned and then have me tell her about herself based on nothing but the scan. She refused to tell me anything about her life experiences. I told her that with our patients, we always try to put the scans in the context of their lives. But she was determined to see what the scan alone would reveal. So, we scanned her, and it showed that the front part of her brain was far more active compared to our healthy group, which correlated with our "persistent" brain type.

"So, tell me about myself," she insisted.

"Well, you are more likely to be persistent and strong-willed, and you are very good at getting things done."

She smiled and said I was right on those points.

"However," I added, "you get upset when things don't go your way, you have a tendency to be stubborn, and you say 'no' a lot."

"No, I don't," she shot back.

"You don't say 'no' a lot?" I asked.

"No, no, no, no, I don't," she said, then paused for a moment and chuckled. "Well, maybe I do tend to say no first."

A BRIEF HISTORY OF PERSONALITY TYPES

Throughout history, there have been many attempts to categorize people and personality. The Greek physician Hippocrates (c. 460 to c. 370 BC) described four fundamental temperaments he believed were caused by an excess or lack of bodily fluids:

- Sanguine (outgoing, social, risk-taking)
- Phlegmatic (relaxed, peaceful, easygoing)
- Choleric (take-charge, decisive, goal-oriented)
- Melancholic (thoughtful, reserved, introverted, sad, anxious)

I have to confess that ever since I was a child, I've been a huge fan of the Charles Schulz *Peanuts* comic strip. I even had Snoopy sheets on my bed (shhh—don't tell anyone!) when I was a young soldier stationed in West Germany. My love for the comic strip stuck with me through college, and I even found a creative way to work it into one of my first psychology homework assignments. For a class on Temperament and Personality, I wrote a paper using the *Peanuts* characters as examples of Hippocrates's four temperament types. Obviously, Snoopy was sanguine, Schroeder phlegmatic, Lucy choleric, and Charlie Brown melancholic. Ever since writing that paper, I have been hooked on looking into the science of how we classify personality.

Teachers, employers, and therapists often use personality tests to help them understand their students, employees, and patients. These are three of the best-known tests:

- **Myers-Briggs**: 16 personality types, based on 4 sets of behaviors— Extroversion vs. Introversion, Sensing vs. Intuition, Thinking vs. Feeling, and Perceiving vs. Judging
- **DISC**: Often used in business, based on 4 traits—Dominance, Influence, Steadiness, and Conscientiousness
- **Big Five**: Based on 5 basic dimensions of personality— Extraversion, Agreeableness, Openness, Conscientiousness, and Neuroticism

These tests give people a sense of uniqueness and belonging, yet, despite their widespread use, there is surprisingly little neuroscience underlying their practical application. Of these tests, the Big Five model is the most widely accepted framework among neuroscientists.

A NEW MODEL BASED ON 160,000 BRAIN SPECT SCANS AND 3 MILLION QUESTIONNAIRES

Over the years, our brain imaging work gained wider recognition as an effective tool to more accurately diagnose and treat people with mental health issues. As a result, an increasing number of people wanted to get a brain scan but either lacked the resources or didn't live close enough to one of our clinics. In an effort to help as many people as possible benefit from what we have learned from our brain imaging work, we developed a series of questionnaires to help people predict what their brains might look like if we could scan them. The questionnaires were based on tens of thousands of scans. Obviously, they didn't have the same level of accuracy as a scan, but they were the next best thing. In the last three decades, thousands of mental health professionals have used our questionnaires in their practices, and they've told us it completely changed the way they think about and help their patients.

In 2014, we created our free online Brain Health Assessment (BHA), which offers insights into your brain type and gives scores on important areas of brain health. As of this writing, more than 3 million people worldwide have taken the BHA at www.brainhealthassessment.com. The questions in the BHA were validated comparing brain region activity to the answers to 300 questions. The most predictive 38 questions were chosen.

Now, after studying more than 160,000 brain SPECT scans, we have identified 5 primary brain types and 11 combination brain types:

Primary Brain Types

Brain Type 1: Balanced
Brain Type 2: Spontaneous
Brain Type 3: Persistent
Brain Type 4: Sensitive
Brain Type 5: Cautious

Combination Brain Types

Brain Type 6: Spontaneous-Persistent
Brain Type 7: Spontaneous-Persistent-Sensitive
Brain Type 8: Spontaneous-Persistent-Sensitive-Cautious
Brain Type 9: Persistent-Sensitive-Cautious
Brain Type 10: Persistent-Sensitive
Brain Type 11: Persistent-Cautious
Brain Type 12: Spontaneous-Persistent-Cautious
Brain Type 13: Spontaneous-Cautious
Brain Type 14: Spontaneous-Sensitive
Brain Type 15: Spontaneous-Sensitive-Cautious
Brain Type 16: Sensitive-Cautious

Knowing your brain type can help you understand more about how you learn, study, and perform in school, as well as how you interact with your teachers, fellow students, and others. It can also help you know how to optimize your individual brain to make you more successful at school. Here is an example:

Maya and Jackie

Maya, 16, was in her junior year of high school and was struggling to keep up with her schoolwork while also studying to take the SAT. Her room at home was a mess and she often couldn't find her notes from class or her SAT prep materials. When she did study, she couldn't stay focused for long and would get distracted by social media, so she was getting behind on things. She started thinking she would never get into college, so why should she even bother studying so hard for the SAT? Her mom, Jackie, was constantly hounding her to study more and work harder and telling her she was being lazy, which only added to Maya's discouragement.

Maya was Brain Type 13 (Spontaneous-Cautious) and had low activity in her prefrontal cortex (associated with attention issues, disorganization, and impulse control problems) combined with increased activity in her basal ganglia and amygdala (a tendency for anxiety and predicting the worst).

Jackie was Brain Type 3 (Persistent) and had above-average activity in the front part of her brain. She was a natural at taking charge and getting things done and expected everybody else to be just as good at powering through their to-do list, so she thought Maya was just being lazy with her study schedule. And Jackie hated it when things were out of place, so she would get angry at Maya for having such a messy room. These negative thoughts would get stuck in Jackie's head, and she would bring up things Maya did wrong years ago, which just added more stress to Maya's situation.

To help, we had to balance both Maya and Jackie's brains using supplements and lifestyle interventions targeted to each individual brain type. After a few weeks, Maya was able to get organized better and stay more focused while studying, which gave her more confidence in her abilities and motivated her to do well so she could get into college. Jackie learned that Maya's brain worked differently from her own and stopped expecting her to tackle her studies the same way she had done when she was that age. And with her own brain calmed down, Jackie stopped getting so upset about things being out of place and quit harping on Maya about things that had happened years earlier.

When it came time for the SAT, Maya did better than she had anticipated and eventually got into her top choice for college. And she and her mom now get along much better, so they are both less stressed in general. Knowing your brain type and the brain type of the important people in your life and can help not only in your schoolwork but also in your relationships.

KNOW YOUR BRAIN TYPE AND THE BRAIN TYPE OF YOUR INNER CIRCLE

To determine your brain type, take the free BHA at www.brainhealthassessment.com and share it with your family and friends at school. It will take only 5 to 7 minutes. Here is a short summary of the 5 primary types.

1. Balanced Brain Type: *Advantages and Challenges of Symmetrical Brain Activity*

One of the most common brain types is the Balanced Brain Type. This group tends to do what they say they're going to do, show up on time, and follow through on tasks they promise to get done. Typically, they dislike risks, are not first adopters, and tended to color within the lines when they were kids. They like rules and tend to stick to them. Because of their high level of conscientiousness and lack of risk-taking behaviors, they tend to live longer.

People with the Balanced Brain Type tend to:	People with the Balanced Brain Type are less likely to:
Be focused	Have a short attention span
Exhibit good impulse control	Be impulsive
Be conscientious	Be unreliable
Be flexible	Be worried
Be positive	Be negative
Be resilient	Be anxious
Be emotionally stable	

Our imaging work shows that people with this brain type tend to have full, even, symmetrical activity throughout the brain, with the most activity in the cerebellum, which is one of the brain's major processing centers.

Balanced Brain Type

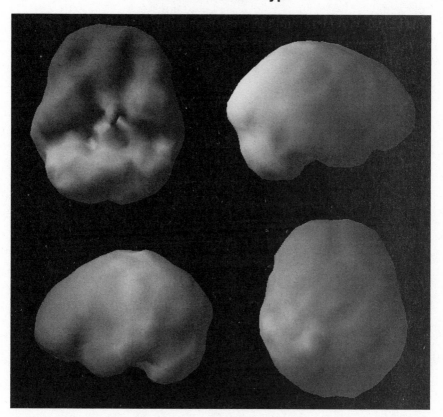

Full, even, symmetrical activity

2. Spontaneous Brain Type: *Advantages and Disadvantages of a Sleepy Prefrontal Cortex*

People with the Spontaneous Brain Type tend to enjoy doing things on the spur of the moment, love trying new things, and often think that rules don't apply to them. They may struggle with organization and can engage in risky behavior.

People with the Spontaneous Brain Type tend to:	People with the Spontaneous Brain Type are less likely to:
Be spontaneous	Hate surprises
Take risks	Avoid risk
Exhibit creative, "out of the box" thinking	Prefer routine
	Like sameness
Be curious	Play by the rules
Have a wide range of interests	Be practical
Like surprises	Exhibit good attention to detail
Be restless	Exhibit good impulse control
Get distracted easily	Be settled
Need to be highly interested to focus	
Struggle with organization	
Arrive late or in a rush to meetings	
Be diagnosed with ADHD	

Our imaging work shows that people with this brain type typically have lower activity in the front part of the brain, in an area called the prefrontal cortex (PFC). When activity in the PFC is too low, it can be troublesome.

Prefrontal Cortex (PFC)

The PFC is the most evolved part of the brain, making up 30 percent of the human brain, 11 percent of the chimpanzee brain (our closest cousin), 7 percent of the dog brain, 3.5 percent of the cat brain (which is why cats need nine lives), and 1 percent of a mouse's brain (which is why they become food for cats). The PFC is your "executive control center," responsible for behaviors that are necessary for you to focus on and achieve your goals. (See the PFC's primary functions in the "Brain Regions: Functions and Problems" chart in chapter 1.)

When the PFC is healthy, people are able to supervise themselves and make good decisions. When it is sleepy or low in activity, they tend to be more spontaneous and creative, take risks, and think outside the

Spontaneous Brain Type

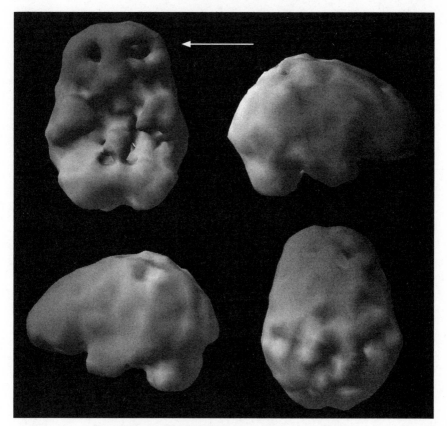

Low prefrontal cortex activity at front of brain
(eee balanced brain type for comparison).

box—which can be good or bad. Whether it is due to medical conditions (such as ADHD, brain trauma, or dementia) or poor lifestyle choices (such as a lack of sleep or excessive alcohol or marijuana use), a less-active PFC makes people tend to struggle. (See the PFC's main problems in the "Brain Regions: Functions and Problems" chart in chapter 1.)

Think of the PFC as the brain's brake. It stops us from saying or doing things that are not in our best interest, but it can also block creativity. The PFC is the little voice in our heads that helps us decide between the banana and the banana split. The Spontaneous Brain Type tends to be associated with lower dopamine levels in the brain, which may cause people to be more restless, to be risk takers, and to need to be very interested in something in order to stay focused.

Our research team has published several studies showing that when people with this brain type try to concentrate, they actually have less activity in the PFC, which causes them to need excitement or stimulation in order to focus (think of firefighters and race car drivers). Smokers and heavy coffee drinkers also tend to fit this type, as they use these substances to turn their brains on.

Optimize the Spontaneous Brain Type

This brain type is best optimized by boosting dopamine levels to strengthen the PFC and avoiding supplements and medications that can lower the already low PFC function, which can then take the brakes off behavior. For example, we have treated many people who had done things they later regretted, such as spending money they did not have, when they were put on antidepressants called selective serotonin reuptake inhibitors (SSRIs). It turned out they had low activity in the PFC, and the serotonin-boosting medications diminished their judgment.

Do	Don't
Eat a higher-protein, lower-carbohydrate diet	Take calming supplements, such as 5-HTP
Engage in physical exercise	Take serotonin-boosting medications, such as SSRIs
Take stimulating supplements, such as green tea, rhodiola, ginseng	

3. Persistent Brain Type: *OCD and Being in Control*

People with the Persistent Brain Type are often take-charge people who won't take no for an answer. They tend to be tenacious and stubborn. In addition, they may worry, have trouble sleeping, be argumentative and oppositional, and hold grudges from the past.

People with the Persistent Brain Type tend to:	People with the Persistent Brain Type are less likely to:
Be persistent	Be ever-changing
Be strong-willed	Be timid
Like routine	Be spontaneous
Be suspicious	Be trusting
Get "stuck" on thoughts	Let go of negativity easily
Hold on to hurts	Let go of hurts easily
See what is wrong	See what is right
Be oppositional or argumentative	Be noncritical
Be more vulnerable to obsessive-compulsive disorder	Be cooperative

Our imaging work shows that people with this brain type often have increased activity in an area in the front part of the brain called the anterior cingulate gyrus (ACG).

Normal "Active" Brain SPECT Scan

Persistent Brain Type

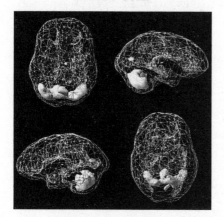

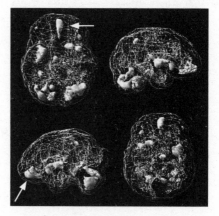

Most active areas in cerebellum at back of brain

High anterior cingulate activity at front of brain (arrows)

Anterior Cingulate Gyrus (ACG)

The ACG runs lengthwise, deep in the frontal lobes of the brain, and is involved with cognitive flexibility. Healthy activity in the ACG helps you go with the flow, adapt to change, cooperate with others, and deal successfully with new problems. The ACG helps you effectively manage change and transitions, which is an essential ingredient in personal, interpersonal, and professional growth. (See the ACG's primary functions in the "Brain Regions: Functions and Problems" chart in chapter 1.)

Increased activity in the ACG is often associated with being strong-willed, wanting things to be just so, perfectionism, and liking routine, which can be good or troublesome. (See the ACG's main problems in the "Brain Regions: Functions and Problems" chart in chapter 1.)

We think of the ACG as the brain's gear shifter. It helps people go from thought to thought or move from action to action. It is involved with being mentally flexible and going with the flow. When the ACG is overactive, usually due to low levels of serotonin, people can have problems shifting attention, which can make them persist, even when it may not be a good idea for them to do so. Caffeine and diet pills tend to worsen this, because this brain type does *not* need more stimulation. People who have this brain type may feel as though they need a glass of wine at night—or two or three—to calm their worries. Be aware, alcohol is *not* a health food, and too much can damage the brain. There are healthier ways to calm the brain.

Optimize the Persistent Brain Type

The best strategy to balance the Persistent Brain Type is to find natural ways to boost serotonin because it is calming to the brain. High-glycemic carbohydrates turn to sugar quickly and increase serotonin, which is why many people become addicted to simple carbohydrates like bread, pasta, and sweets. These "mood foods" are often used to self-medicate an underlying mood issue. Avoid these quick fixes, because they can cause long-term health problems.

Do	Don't
Engage in physical exercise	Eat high-glycemic carbohydrates
Take calming supplements, such 5-HTP, saffron	(bread, pasta, sweets)

4. Sensitive Brain Type: *Sadness and Empathy*

People with the Sensitive Brain Type tend to feel deeply about their family, friends, and all fellow humans and are more likely to have lots of automatic negative thoughts (ANTs) and low moods.

People with the Sensitive Brain Type tend to:	People with the Sensitive Brain Type are less likely to:
Be sensitive	Be emotionally reserved
Be deeply feeling	Be superficial
Have great empathy	Be consistently happy
Struggle with moods	Have little empathy
Be prone to pessimism	Have positive thoughts
Have lots of ANTs (automatic negative thoughts)	Have few ANTs
Have depression	

Our imaging work shows that people with this brain type often have increased activity in the limbic or emotional areas of the brain.

Normal "Active" Brain
SPECT Scan

Sensitive Brain Type

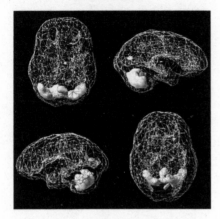

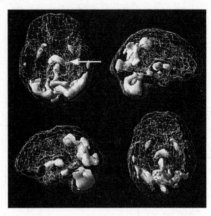

Most active areas in
cerebellum at back of brain

High deep limbic activity (arrow)

Limbic System

The limbic system is one of the most interesting and critical parts of being human and is packed with functions—all of which are critical for human behavior and survival. It sets the emotional tone of the mind and modulates motivation. (See the limbic system's primary functions in the "Brain Regions: Functions and Problems" chart in chapter 1.)

Our experience at Amen Clinics tells us that when the limbic system is less active, there is generally a more positive and hopeful state of mind. However, when the limbic system is working too hard, it is often associated with sadness, negative thinking, and negative emotions. (See the limbic system's main problems in the "Brain Regions: Functions and Problems" chart in chapter 1.)

Optimize the Sensitive Brain Type

Engaging in activities that release feel-good neurotransmitters, eliminating negative thoughts, and taking certain supplements can help people with the Sensitive Brain Type. If someone with this type is also a Persistent Brain Type, the supplements or medications that boost serotonin may help the best.

Do	Don't
Engage in physical exercise	Be a couch potato
Practice ANT therapy (see	Let your thoughts run wild
chapter 14)	Focus on the negative
Practice gratitude	
Take supplements, such as	
omega-3 fatty acids, SAMe,	
vitamin D	

5. Cautious Brain Type: *Some Anxiety Is Good for You*

People with the Cautious Brain Type tend to struggle more with anxiety, which causes them to be more cautious and reserved. On the flip side, it makes them more prepared.

People with the Cautious Brain Type tend to:	People with the Cautious Brain Type are less likely to:
Be prepared	Be unconcerned about being
Be cautious	fully prepared
Avoid risk	Take risks
Be motivated	Be calm
Be reserved	Relax easily
Have a busy mind	Have a quiet mind
Be temperamental	Be even-tempered
Have difficulty relaxing	Feel secure
Have anxiety	

On SPECT images, we often see heightened activity in the anxiety centers of the brain, such as the basal ganglia, amygdala, and insular cortex. People with this brain type also tend to have low levels of the neurotransmitter GABA.

Normal "Active" Brain   Cautious Brain Type
SPECT Scan

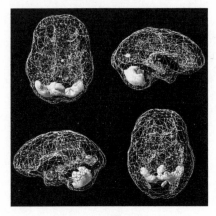
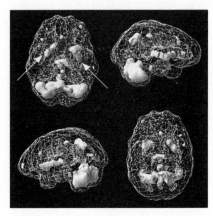

Most active areas in   High basal ganglia activity (arrows)
cerebellum at back of brain

Basal Ganglia, Amygdala, and Insular Cortex

The basal ganglia, amygdala, and insular cortex are structures toward the center of the brain that surround the limbic system. They are essential to healthy human functioning because they set the body's anxiety level, control motivation and drive, and are involved in forming habits. (See the basal ganglia's primary functions in the "Brain Regions: Functions and Problems" chart in chapter 1.)

The basal ganglia are connected with other areas of the brain and are involved with integrating feelings, thoughts and movement. When the basal ganglia are overactive or underactive, a number of problems can arise, including anxiety and a tendency to predict the worst. (See the basal ganglia's main problems in the "Brain Regions: Functions and Problems" chart in chapter 1.)

A certain amount of anxiety is healthy and necessary in order to help us make good decisions and keep us out of trouble. And, while we all may experience basal ganglia symptoms occasionally, having an issue like chronic, unremitting worry is not normal and can be very distressing.

Optimizing the Cautious Brain Type

This brain type is best optimized by finding ways to soothe the brain while avoiding things that worsen feelings of anxiety.

Do	Don't
Practice meditation	Ingest caffeine
Practice hypnosis	Drink alcohol
Take supplements, such as vitamin B$_6$, magnesium, GABA	

Note that alcohol may decrease anxiety in the short term, but withdrawal from alcohol causes anxiety and places a person with anxiety at greater risk for alcohol addiction.

Combination Brain Types: *Most of Us*

It is common to have more than one brain type. If you have a combination brain type, use a combination of the optimization strategies to boost your brain health. To determine if you have a combination brain type, take the free BHA at www.brainhealthassessment.com.

3

CHANGING HABITS

How to Swap Old Ways for Smarter Strategies

Changing your study habits is a critical step toward becoming a more effective student. It is also the foundational element that will help you get the most out of the rest of this book. The process of change involves five things. I like to use the mnemonic, or memory device, STAMP to make it easy to remember, because these five behaviors are far greater than the sum of their parts:

- Set yourself up to win
- Tools
- Attitude
- Motivation
- Perseverance

SET YOURSELF UP TO WIN

Start off slowly, at a pace that is easy to handle. If you haven't been to school for ten years, don't expect to successfully complete 24 college units your first semester. Likewise, don't overexert yourself right off the bat, or you may run out of energy quickly. The same way a long-distance runner will build up muscles slowly, so should you build up your academic

HOW THE BRAIN CREATES HABITS AND HOW YOU CAN REWIRE YOUR BRAIN

Your brain has roughly 100 billion neurons, and every time you have a thought to take an action, some of those neurons fire with activity. If you keep repeating the same activity over and over or keep having the same thoughts, your neurons keep firing together until they begin wiring together in a process called long-term potentiation (LTP). With this process, whether what you are doing or thinking is productive or unproductive for you, networks of your brain cells create connections to automate that behavior. At first, the connections are fragile, but with repetition over time, this neural circuitry becomes very strong and the behaviors become *potentiated*. Basically, they become habits. Depending on what you've taught your brain to do, the LTP process can either help you be a better student or make it much harder for you.

The good news is, you can rewire your brain and change your behaviors. Getting adequate sleep, exercising on a regular basis, and resisting the urge to scroll through your social media pages at all hours will help shore up your brain's willpower circuitry. Every time you replace an old, unproductive habit with a more productive one, your brain will overwrite those old connections and start building a neural superhighway to success.

tolerance. If you start too fast, you'll end up like the runner who tries to go five miles after a two-year layoff. The runner will have torn muscles, and you'll have a shattered ego.

In setting yourself up to succeed, you also need to learn how to take well-planned risks. If you have confidence in your abilities, you can push yourself to academic heights that have always been beyond your grasp. But the only way to gain that confidence is by taking risks and winning at them most of the time. If you don't take a chance on yourself, you'll never know your capabilities. The first time you successfully challenge another student or even a teacher because you know the correct answer, your confidence will start to build.

When you take a risk and succeed—when you ace a tough calculus test, write a killer English essay, or get a great grade on a chemistry project—your brain releases dopamine, a neurotransmitter that triggers good feelings. Healthy dopamine levels promote feelings of pleasure, motivation, and focus. This elevated mood ultimately helps you be even more successful.

Even so, I know it isn't easy to take a risk. You may be thinking, "What if I'm wrong?" To which I say, "So what?" You'll certainly never forget the correct answer and at least you will have tried. I have heard many students say that they gave up on their dreams of becoming a doctor, lawyer, journalist, or engineer because they didn't think they had the smarts for it. This is usually not true. If you follow the principles in this book and take a systematic approach to study and to your career goals, then you can succeed! You won't accomplish anything, however, without risking some time, money, and pride. But as you'll discover, it's so worth it!

Here's a quick tip to set yourself up to win from the get-go each day. Start with a good attitude in your first class so you'll do well from the beginning of your day. You'll feel good about your accomplishments, and you'll want to experience that feeling again. This will spur you on! If you neglect to prepare for your first class of the day, you'll be continually behind and feel inadequate. Since no one likes to feel that way, you might end up dropping out to rid yourself of the feeling. If you continually place yourself in depressing or losing situations, you will not win. If you come to class prepared, however, you'll be able to participate and be encouraged to prepare more often. This concept in life is invaluable. Success breeds success. If you set yourself up to win, you'll win!

TOOLS: ONLY THE BEST WILL DO

To do something right, you need the proper tools. Where would a surgeon be without a scalpel, retractors, and scrub nurse? What if a construction worker showed up at a job site with no hammer, nails, or wood? There's no way they could do their job. This book will help you take stock of the necessary tools for study and will offer many practical aids for sharpening these tools. Any good grocery store owner knows their inventory, and so should you. You need to know what you've got in stock and what you're missing.

Exercise: Take a few minutes to write out five strengths and five weaknesses that you have regarding your study skills. If you know your strengths and weaknesses, you will be able to improve your weak areas and build on the strong ones.

My Strengths

1. _____

_____

2. _____

_____

3. _____

_____

4. _____

_____

5. _____

_____

My Weaknesses

1. _____

_____

2. _____

_____

3. _____

_____

4. _____

_____

5. _____

_____

Throughout the rest of this book, you'll discover the tools you need to turn your weaknesses into strengths. Be sure to practice and review your study skills often. The more you practice good study habits, the more your brain will lay down and strengthen neural pathways to make those behaviors automatic. Eventually, good study habits will feel completely natural to you.

ATTITUDE: DOES YOURS NEED AN ADJUSTMENT?

Your attitude toward your schoolwork will be either a motivating force or a constant drag on your energy. Approach the learning process with the idea of gaining the most that you can; it is the only rational way to spend your time. If you're constantly looking beyond what you're studying, or you view it as purposeless, you'll slow your progress and lengthen the time it takes you to reach your goal. If, on the other hand, you concentrate on preparing for your classes and milking them for everything they're worth, you'll find that studying afterward will go faster. In addition, if you challenge yourself to find value in everything you learn, you can find ways to use that knowledge to aid you in further studies.

As you adopt new habits, you must assume an attitude of confidence. Believing in your ability to achieve is paramount to success. One of the best ways to enhance self-confidence is to surround yourself with people who believe in your abilities and build you up. Friends, family, and professors who are on your "team" and are rooting for you increase your chances of success.

Stay away from people who are constantly putting you down, telling you that the field of your choice is too competitive, or that you're not smart enough to succeed. During my sophomore year of college, after I had decided to go to medical school, my speech teacher told me that her younger brother didn't get into medical school even though, according to her, he was twice as smart as me! In other words, she was telling me I didn't have a chance. Fortunately, I was smart enough to realize I didn't need this kind of discouragement, so I quickly cut off most of my communication with her. If I had listened to her long enough, I just might have started to believe her, and I might have given up hope of going to medical school.

On the other side of the spectrum, as I talked to my father about the medical school adventure, he told me that I could do anything I set my mind to. You know, he was right! Of course, I had setbacks like everyone else. I remember times when I would get emotionally down about the pressures or workload at school. In those times, my dad would take me by the shoulders, look me in the eye, and say, "Son, you're going to make it." Then he would give me a quick shake and tell me to straighten up. Thank God I had his confidence to lean on when mine was weak! Where would I be if I had listened to those who did not believe in me? I hate to think of it.

I can't stress enough the importance of surrounding yourself with people who see your potential and exude an attitude of confidence. Hanging out with people who are motivated and have a clear path to their goals will inspire you to do the same. Plus, it makes it seem much easier every step of the way if you see someone else doing it too.

TECH TIP FROM CHLOE AND ALIZÉ

Tell Siri, Alexa, or whatever tech personal assistant you have to give you encouragement at regular intervals throughout the day or right before a big test. A simple "You're doing great!" can really help.

MOTIVATION: HOW TO FIND YOURS

In order to be a better student, it is critical for you to know *why* it is important. You'll be more likely to perform at your peak if you have insight into what fuels your engine.

What drives your desire to be a more successful student?

- Are you a high school student who wants to go to a prestigious university?

- Are you a sophomore pre-medical student who needs an A in organic chemistry to make it into medical school so you can fulfill your dream of becoming a doctor?
- Are you a junior psychology major who needs to finish with very good grades to have a chance at a competitive graduate school so you can earn a PhD and become a psychologist as you've always wanted?
- Are you a business student who wants to prepare the best possible résumé so you can land a high-paying corporate job upon graduation?
- Are you returning to school so you can make a career change that will be more fulfilling on a personal level?
- Are you doing on-the-job training so you can get a promotion that will allow you to take better care of your family?
- Are you a student who just wants to get better grades and learn more while expending less energy?
- Are you hoping that being a more successful student will help you feel more confident about yourself?

Exercise: Too many people are thrown around by the whims of the day, rather than using their brains to plan their lives and follow through on their goals. One of the best ways to figure out what motivates you is to write it down. Tell your brain what you want and let your brain help you match your behavior to get it! When you focus on negativity, you will feel depressed. If you focus on fear, you are likely to feel anxious. If you focus on achieving your goals, you are much more likely to succeed.

I have designed a powerful yet simple motivation exercise called the ONE PAGE MIRACLE to help guide your thoughts, words, and actions. I've seen this exercise quickly focus and change many people's lives.

Directions: On the following form, clearly write out your major goals, in the following areas:

Relationships: parents, siblings, significant other, children, friends, extended family

School and Work: short- and long-term education and career goals

Finances: short- and long-term financial goals

Self: emotional and physical health, personal interests, spirituality

Work on these goals over time. After you finish your initial draft, I want you to look at your ONE PAGE MIRACLE every day, and then before you do or say anything, I want you to ask yourself, "Is my behavior getting me what I want?"

If you focus on your goals every day, it becomes much easier for you to match your behavior to get what you want. Your life becomes more conscious and you spend energy on goals that are important to you.

The areas of relationships, school/work, finances, and self are separated in order to encourage a more balanced approach to life. Burnout occurs when our lives become unbalanced and we overextend ourselves in one area while ignoring another. For example, in one's teens, spending excessive time with friends can lead to school failure and family stress.

MY ONE PAGE MIRACLE

What Do I Want? What Am I Doing to Make It Happen?

Relationships

Parents: _____

_____

_____

Siblings: _____

_____

_____

Significant Other: _____

_____

_____

Children: _____

_____

_____

Friends: _____

_____

_____

Family: _____

_____

_____

School

_____

_____

_____

Work

_____

_____

_____

Finances

_____

_____

_____

Self

Emotional Health: _____
_____
_____

Physical Health: _____
_____
_____

Personal Interests: _____
_____
_____

Spirituality: _____
_____
_____

Let your brain help you design and implement your life. Work toward goals that are important to you. Many other people or corporations are happy to decide what you should do with your life, but you can use the ONE PAGE MIRACLE to help you be the one who has the say. Your brain receives and creates reality. Give it some direction to help make your life what you want it to be.

Anchor Images

Did you know that 50 percent of your brain is dedicated to vision? Because of this, it can be very helpful to surround yourself with what I like to call "anchor images" that remind you why you want to be a more successful student. These images can shift your motivation into high gear. If you want to be a more effective student so you can get into a particular university, use a picture of that university as your computer background so every time you turn it on, you're reminded of why you're studying. If you're going back to school to land a better job so you can support your family, post your

EXAMPLE: JORDAN'S ONE PAGE MIRACLE

What Do I Want? What Am I Doing to Make It Happen?

Relationships

Parents: <u>I want to be close to my parents.</u>
<u>I want to have open communication and mutual respect.</u>

Siblings: <u>I want to be more patient with my brother and do things</u>
<u>together.</u>

Significant other: <u>I want to have someone in my life who encourages</u>
<u>me to be my best.</u>

Children: <u>I don't have kids now, but when I do, I want to set a good</u>
<u>example.</u>

Friends: <u>I want to continue to spend time with special friends, espe-</u>
<u>cially those that have my same values.</u>

Family: <u>I want to stay involved with other members of my family in</u>
<u>a positive way.</u>

School

<u>I want to work hard to be a good student to give myself the most</u>
<u>options for college.</u>
<u>I want to be a respectful student and strive to have good relationships</u>
<u>with my teachers.</u>

Work

I want to have a job by age 16 to earn my own money.
I want to work in fields that are interesting to help me decide what career I might want to go into.

Finances

I want to spend whatever money I have wisely, but save enough to also have fun.
I want to learn how to manage money.

Self

Emotional health: I want to feel stable, focused, and happy and not be upset by little things.
I want to feel positive and optimistic.

Physical health: I want to eat a diet that helps me feel better and live longer.
I want to walk 30 minutes every day.

Personal interests: I want to continue following the news to keep up on current events.
I love playing word games and want to get better at them.

Spirituality: I strive to live a life pleasing to God.
I go to church to have a group of people with whom to worship and pray.

favorite picture of your family in plain view to anchor you. If you want to study more efficiently in less time so you can enjoy other pursuits—playing guitar, playing tennis, making movies—put up pictures of yourself doing those things.

Don't forget that motivation is your business! In higher education, you'll encounter very little encouragement to prompt you to do your best work. It's up to you to keep yourself inspired to thrive. Come up with fun ways to motivate yourself, such as rewarding yourself for consistently maintaining your new habits, finding entertaining ways to study (at the park or beach), or getting a friend to hit the books with you.

> ☐
> **TECH TIP FROM CHLOE AND ALIZÉ**
> We set our phone calendars so that every time we turn them on, a reminder to view our ONE PAGE MIRACLE pops up. It keeps us inspired and reminds us why we want to study effectively.

After you have formulated your goals, make a conscious decision to change your methods for reaching them. That's right: Decide to change! This decision will be the pivotal point in your academic career. After you make the confident decision to make it happen, you need to act on it right away. The sooner you put your focus in the direction you want to go, the more consistent you will be and the more likely you will be to succeed.

A simple strategy you can use to stay on track with your new habits is something I call "then what?" These are the two most powerful words when it comes to your success as a student, and keeping them at the top of your mind can literally change your performance in a positive way. If I do this, *then what* will happen? If I take sloppy notes, *then what* will happen? If I take notes that are easy to read, *then what*? If I skip a lecture, fail to prepare for class, or cram at the last minute, *then what*? If I pay close attention in class, *then what*? Will any of these actions help me with any of my goals? Think about the consequences of your behavior before you act.

KEEP YOUR LIMBIC SYSTEM HEALTHY FOR HEALTHY MOTIVATION

The brain's limbic system influences your motivation and drive. When activity in the limbic system is optimal, it's what gets you to hop out of bed in the morning and keep powering through your day. Brain imaging shows that when there is overactivity in this brain system, it is associated with a drop in motivation and drive, which is commonly linked to depression. Here are a few strategies to enhance the health of the limbic system:

- Engage in physical exercise.
- Practice ANT therapy (see chapter 14 to learn this simple technique).
- Try mood-boosting supplements, such as omega-3 fatty acids and SAMe.

PERSEVERANCE

In order to change bad study habits or patterns, you must develop perseverance. Many people in every walk of life never reach their full potential, not due to a lack of talent or intelligence, but rather because of a lack of tenacity. You need to understand two concepts before you'll be able to power up your perseverance:

1. You need to count the cost beforehand.
2. You'll experience a certain amount of pain before you reach your goal.

Jesus said, "Suppose one of you wants to build a tower. Will he not first sit down and estimate the cost to see if he has enough money to complete it? For if he lays the foundation and is not able to finish it, everyone who sees it will ridicule him, saying, 'This fellow began to build and was not able to finish.'" (Luke 14:28)

In order to persevere, you must know what you're up against. If you count the cost of the goals you're pursuing, you'll be less likely to start something that you'll later drop—which would surely make you feel like a failure. For example, if your goal is to become a heart surgeon, you need to be fully aware that this will require:

- a four-year undergraduate degree with a major like biology
- good scores on the MCAT
- four years of medical school
- about five years of general surgery residency training
- about two years of specialized heart surgery residency training
- passing the licensing exam
- obtaining board certification

Phew! This adds up to about 15 years of study to attain your goal. Ask yourself if you're willing to invest 15 years of your life before reaping the benefits of your efforts. And be honest with yourself! If you have other conflicting life goals that are important to you, you may need to rethink this goal. Perhaps if being a heart surgeon doesn't fit into your overall life goals, then another career in the medical field would give you the job satisfaction you're seeking while letting you achieve a more balanced life.

Perseverance also requires a dose of pain. American society seems to promote the assumption that all pain is bad. I find, however, that not all pain is bad—and indeed, in many instances, pain is a necessary ingredient for personal growth.

Growth and change involve pain. There were many nights when my first son, Anton, awakened in the night moaning from the pain in his legs. As I massaged his little legs or placed a cool, wet cloth upon them, the growing pains would subside. Anton learned to accept the pain of physical growth, because it fit into his desire to be as tall as his grandfather, who is six feet four inches.

There is pain in any learning situation. You will experience the pain of hard work and long nights, studying when your friends are playing, postponing material or social goals for academic ones, and doing poorly on an exam even though you studied hard for it because the teacher asked "off the wall" questions. Prepare yourself for the pain and accept its place in your personal life and in your study life. Learning to use the curveballs to your advantage is so important, because they are certainly not going to stop anytime soon. In fact, after you've finished school and joined the workforce, that's when they really come at you. But it's up to you to decide if these setbacks throw you for a loop and break you down or if they inspire you to think fast on your feet and make you stronger. If you aren't willing to accept some pain in your life, then you will revert to old habits or drop out whenever the going gets tough.

It takes time to develop good study habits, just as it takes time for any medicine to work after you have taken it. If you do not take your medicine as prescribed, its effects will be compromised. Likewise, if you lack persistence in applying the tools that I will help you develop and sharpen, then this book will have little impact on you.

CHANGE YOUR BRAIN, CHANGE YOUR GRADES: CHANGING HABITS

- Set yourself up to succeed by starting at a reasonable pace and taking well-planned risks. Give yourself positive, reinforcing experiences. This is the key to having the confidence of a winner.
- Obtain the tools for change and update them regularly.
- Use your attitude to fuel change and surround yourself with people who believe in your potential.
- Find out what motivates you to study better and decide to change bad study habits.
- Develop the perseverance to change by counting the cost of your endeavors beforehand and accepting that pain is a necessary part of change and growth.
- Know the six stages of change and understand that slipups are normal.

THE 6 STAGES OF CHANGE

It takes time to rewire your brain. Being aware of the fact that your brain goes through six stages of change can help you stay on track when adopting habits that will make you a better student.

- *Stage 1: I Won't or I Can't:* In this stage, the downsides of change appear to outweigh the benefits. If you're in this stage, ask yourself several times a day, "If I decided to change, how would it benefit me?" This helps your brain focus on the benefits of change.
- *Stage 2: I Might:* You may still feel ambivalent about changing. To push yourself in the right direction, ask yourself, "If I decided to change, what are the first steps I could take?"
- *Stage 3: I Will:* By now, you see that that the benefits of changing outweigh the downsides and you begin developing a plan.
- *Stage 4: I Am:* You are taking action to make change happen, which kick-starts the long-term potentiation (LTP) process and begins to rewire your brain.
- *Stage 5: I Still Am:* LTP is firmly underway, and your new behaviors are beginning to feel reflexive or automatic. But beware that you can still slip back into old habits if you don't make a concerted effort to stick with your new ways.
- *Stage 6: Whoops!* It is completely normal to experience a few slipups as you change your habits. Just ease back into whichever stage you land in.

4

IN THE BEGINNING

PREPARATION FOR LEARNING

In the beginning God created humans. Right? No, that is wrong! In the beginning God created the heavens and the earth. Then he proceeded to create the day and the night, the sun, the moon and the stars, the land and the sea, the forests and the gardens, the fish, the birds and the mammals, etc. He took into account all that was necessary, and he prepared extensively for his ultimate purpose—the creation of humans. (Maybe he took into account more than was necessary; who needs leeches and stink bugs?)

Whether or not you accept the above description on the history of our genesis is not the point. What is important is to recognize that preparation is paramount to accomplishment. With a solid foundation, goals become achievable; without it—impossible!

If you want to become a more successful student, where do you start? Where else but at the beginning? If you want to study writing, you need to learn grammar and vocabulary. If you want to enter the business world, you need to learn mathematics and accounting skills. If you want to be a physician, you should start with basic chemistry and physics. And if you want to be a minister, begin with the Bible and learn public speaking techniques.

To carry this point even further, it is necessary to start at the beginning of the beginning. I know this sounds redundant, but this simple principle will save you many hours of frustration and stress. In chemistry it is essential to know that gold is a metal before you can possibly understand how it reacts to heat. You must know the functions of verbs and prepositions before putting together sentences for a short story. It is essential in psychology or medicine to understand what is normal before you can comprehend what is abnormal.

These four strategies have been proven to help you prepare for learning so that you can be more successful.

1. HONE YOUR READING SKILLS.

Regardless of what grade you're in or what field you're studying, reading skills are essential to a successful academic career. I will not dwell on the mechanics of good reading in this guidebook because most middle schools, high schools, and colleges offer elective courses in reading skills. If your skills could use a boost, I highly recommend such a course. I will, however, offer a few simple observations on reading. Reading for pleasure and reading for study are two completely different animals. One usually takes on the feeling of a warm, cuddly puppy, while the other often resembles a vile cockroach.

Become a word whiz. When reading to learn, be sure to look up words you don't know. This habit will build your vocabulary rapidly and increase your knowledge of the subject.

Don't skip the good stuff. Some people tend to gloss over the charts, graphs, illustrations,

**TECH TIP FROM
CHLOE AND ALIZÉ**
Download a free dictionary app, such as Merriam-Webster, so you can look up words on your smartphone while you read. You can also ask Siri, Alexa, or another personal assistant for the definitions of words you don't know, but be aware that their responses can sometimes be unpredictable. When writing essays, you can also ask them for help with spelling.

italicized words, sidebars, and summary statements included in many textbooks. This is a big mistake! These elements often include critical information that will improve your comprehension and ensure that you the see "the big picture." In the same vein, it's very important to read the preface, table of contents, introduction, and introductory chapters of textbooks. These give you valuable information that is often overlooked by students, who end up struggling without realizing why.

These sections present information on how to use the textbook efficiently, how to study the subject, unique features of the book, why the subject is important, and interesting biographies of the authors that can make the subject matter less impersonal. Reading this part of the text familiarizes you with the task ahead, while giving you an early opportunity to return the book and drop out of the class if it is not what you expected. For example, when I was a junior in college, I enrolled in a biochemistry course I thought would be helpful in my medical education. After reading the preface, introduction, and first two chapters of the text, I found out quickly that I did not want to put myself through that kind of pain twice, since I would have to take a similar class in medical school. I dropped the class and took a course on death and dying, which, although more morbid, was vastly more interesting.

Try to enjoy what you're reading and consider its value to you. I know that this is not always possible, and I have spent more time than I care to admit reading words that seem to have been put together purposely to torment my moods and obscure my thoughts. If you take a broader view and try to see its value, however, it will be easier to wade through the material.

Have a (realistic) plan and stick to it. Decide ahead of time what you want to accomplish when you have finished a section so you can read with a purpose. It is a good practice (in life as well as in reading!) to keep a running tab of where you are and where you are heading. If you follow a plan, you'll find that you waste less time, and unproductive time is what you want to completely eliminate. Be realistic about your plan, though. Don't pressure yourself to digest 10 chapters of a dense economics book in a single sitting. That's just going to set you up for failure. Schedule your time realistically, and you'll absorb the material faster and feel more successful.

When you feel lost, start over. Do you ever find yourself in the middle of a textbook and suddenly realize you have no idea what you've just read? When you're reading and begin to feel lost, stop and ask yourself, "When did I first feel lost?" Then go back to that point and begin reading again until you understand. And this time, try getting through the material without any distractions—like checking your Instagram feed (cough, cough). If you don't start over and simply continue to read without understanding, it will be much tougher and more time-consuming for you to learn the material. When you're feeling lost, the sooner you go back, the better it will be for you, your spouse, your children, your friends, and even your dog, because you will be less irritable.

Got it! A very important statement is repeated several times in the book of Genesis. At the end of each day in creation, God said, "and it was good." Make sure you can say the same thing after each section you study: "It is good. I understand it." If you find yourself saying, "It is *not* good. I have no clue what this is about," start over at the beginning of your lesson until you feel comfortable with the material.

Limit distractions and stop trying to multitask. You may think that multitasking is the key to being a more productive and successful student because you can get more done in less time. But brain studies show that it is very difficult to concentrate well on more than one thing at a time. Researchers at Stanford University have found that rather than being a time-saver, multitasking is actually bad for your brain and makes it harder to sort out relevant information from irrelevant data.[1] Your brain performs better if you focus on one thing at a time. This means you need to limit distractions—no cell phones, no TV, no YouTube. I promise you, the memes can wait.

TECH TIP FROM CHLOE AND ALIZÉ

When you need to read a book for school or on-the-job training, put your cell phone on silent mode and resist the temptation to scroll through your social media feed.

2. CREATE AN IDEAL STUDY ENVIRONMENT.

To study effectively, you need your own private haven. What sort of surroundings help make your study sessions more efficient? Most of what you'll read here involves common sense, but as I have found, common sense is not always a prerequisite for higher learning.

Find a place that is comfortable and quiet. You want it to be comfortable because if you feel good physically, you'll be able to study longer; you want it to be quiet because you need to concentrate! See to it that your chair is comfortable, but not to the extent of encouraging you to fantasize that it is a first-class seat aboard a plane bound for Honolulu. Do not study on your bed! The message you are sending to your brain when you are lying down—to power down—is the opposite of your purpose. You need your brain to be alert and ready to learn (unless, of course, you happen to be taking a class on the interpretation of dreams).

Keep it cool, but not too cool. Studies show that students perform better on tests in rooms that are well ventilated and temperature controlled. A space that is too stuffy, too hot, or too cold can be detrimental to performance. The optimum temperature appears to be in the range of 70 to 78 degrees Fahrenheit.[2]

Let there be light. Make sure that the lighting is good and that it shines over the opposite shoulder of your writing arm. This will diminish unnecessary shadows. Also ensure that the light can be easily adjusted to reduce the glare from glossy textbook pages or your computer screen. If you tend to study at night, be aware that the blue light emitted from the LED screen of your laptop or tablet can mess with your biological rhythms. A 2015 study in the *Proceedings of the National Academy of Science* found that using light-emitting reading devices—like your Kindle, Nook, or iPad—before bedtime prolongs the time it takes to fall asleep, disrupts circadian

---

TECH TIP FROM CHLOE AND ALIZÉ

If you have to study at night (as most students do), check out screen covers or goggles that filter blue light.

rhythms, suppresses melatonin production, reduces the amount of REM sleep, and lowers alertness the following morning.[3]

Make room. Clear your desk, table, or study area to give yourself plenty of room to spread out, so you don't feel cluttered. Only the material you're studying at the moment should be out on your workspace. All other homework should be out of sight. For example, don't study for your English exam with your math homework within eyesight.

Tune in to the right music. There are varying opinions on listening to music during study time. In my experience, listening to soft, instrumental music may enhance a study session. It is obvious, however, that loud, aggressive music—think heavy metal—will not help you assimilate the details of fine art in the Baroque period! And avoid anything that you can't sit still and listen to (for Chloe and Alize, that would be Drake, JB, or the entire *Mamma Mia* soundtrack). If you're one of those students who finds any music distracting, turn it off and let the silence help you concentrate.

Be prepared. If you're going to use any study aids, be sure to have them at hand before you sit down to study so you won't have to interrupt yourself.

3. STAY FRESH AND ENERGIZED.

Take regular breaks. You might think that powering through a study session without taking a break is the best way to get more done. Think again. A 2011 study in the journal *Cognition* found that short breaks allow people to stay focused on a task and avoid the decline in concentration that usually comes over time.[4] Brief breaks allow you to clear your mind so you can come back to the material feeling refreshed and energized. If you're an overachiever, you may balk at the idea of breaks, but just remember that even the bagger at the grocery store down the street gets a 10-minute break every few hours. You should take at least that much time, preferably 10 minutes every hour. There is good reason why psychiatrists see patients for only 50 minutes. Take the hint and give yourself a break—unless, of course, you are the type to take a 50-minute break for every 10 minutes of study.

Get moving. Sitting at your desk for hours on end can be a drag, and it's terrible for your posture. Every time you take a break, get up out of your chair and get your blood pumping. Do a few jumping jacks, stretch, or go for a quick walk outside. It will boost your energy and your mood.

4. DON'T TAKE ADVANCED CLASSES BEFORE MASTERING THE BASICS.

As you have no doubt already noticed, most class material "pyramids"— that is, it builds upon a base of knowledge. Jesus said in the New Testament that a wise man builds his house on a foundation of rock, for it will survive the wind, the rain, and the exposure to time. But it is the foolish man who builds his house on a foundation of sand, for when the winds blow and the rains come, it will quickly crumble. (Matthew 7:24) What you need to do to is build your education on a foundation of rock, so you will have a lot less work to do in the future.

This means you need to make sure you have mastered the necessary prerequisites for the courses you are about to undertake, or your grade might find itself at the undertaker. I remember my first week of general chemistry in college—I was so lost that I thought I was in the wrong room taking a Russian language class. I had taken the prerequisite chemistry class in high school but had barely squeaked by with a C. (I, of course, placed the blame on my girlfriend at that time, who was taking up most of my time and energy.) The smartest thing I did for my career was to drop that class and take a beginning chemistry course instead. It gave me a solid foundation and adequate preparation for the more advanced chemistry classes.

This principle may delay your plans by a few months, but inadequate background and preparation are the major reasons why students drop out of tough programs. So be a good scout and "Be Prepared" for what you are to encounter.

CHANGE YOUR BRAIN, CHANGE YOUR GRADES: PREPARATION FOR LEARNING

- Preparing to learn is paramount to accomplishment.
- Prime your brain for learning.
- Start at the beginning and solidify your academic foundation before you move ahead to more advanced courses.
- Polish your reading skills by using a dictionary app and comprehension aids. Recognize the value in what you read and have a purpose when reading by creating and following a realistic plan. Read the introductory materials of your texts. Avoid distractions.
- Create a comfortable and quiet study environment by keeping the room at a good temperature and by having good light, a comfortable chair, and enough space to work. Remember to keep distractions out of sight and opt for soft music rather than hard rock.
- Stay fresh and energized by taking regular breaks with brief bouts of movement.

5

THE BIG PICTURE

From Generalizations to Specifics

When I first began tutoring in my sophomore year of college, I was amazed to discover that some of my pupils could remember facts I had never even heard. I figured the only reason why I was the tutor and they were the tutees was that I knew where the facts belonged and could put them into a rational sequence. Their facts were often left hanging like leaves without branches to support them.

If I was surprised by this in college, I was astounded in medical school to find a very similar situation of dangling facts. You would think that medical students would have it all together when it comes to having good study habits and knowing the importance of getting the "big picture" before knowing the details. Boy, what naivete! To my shock and dismay, I found the study skills of many medical students on a par with trained monkeys who learned information only after numerous repetitions. It is true that the average intelligence of the medical students with whom I had contact was quite high, but they had wasted literally thousands of hours on circular, repetitive, and unproductive study. I wonder what great medical discoveries could have been made if they had those hours back, but as the Apostle Paul said, "Forgetting that which is behind and straining toward what is ahead, I press on toward the high mark." (Phil. 3:13) That, in fact, is part of what this book is all about: getting high marks.

LOOK FOR THE "BIG PICTURE" FIRST

I think getting the "big picture" in a subject is the first step to being a successful student, but it is a step that far too many ignore. Now, I know many of you are expecting me to tell you that you are having trouble seeing the forest for the trees, which is most likely the case. As you know, if you do not realize that you are in a forest, it is very easy to get lost in the maze of trees and foliage that surrounds you. If, however, you do know where you are and what you are doing there, the forest can be a wonderful place.

Another analogy, that of a trip I once made, will be useful in driving this point home (or, as happened to me, driving me *farther* from home). I was traveling from California to Oklahoma. I had made this trip four or five times before, always driving from Los Angeles to Needles to Flagstaff, and so on. This particular time, however, I was entering my junior year in medical school and must have felt the extraordinary powers of my position in life when I decided that there must be a quicker way to Flagstaff than through Needles. After all, what did the Auto Club (which had mapped out the trip for me—remember, this was long before GPS!) know that a third-year medical student did not?

As I eyed the map, I saw a shortcut from Blythe, California, to Flagstaff, Arizona, saving about two inches on the map. The only difference was the shortcut had a single red line instead of a double green line and it looked a little curvy. I didn't know what the red and green lines meant, but it seemed like a no-brainer to me, so I headed for the shortcut at about 9:30 p.m., expecting to arrive in Flagstaff about 2 o'clock that morning. As you may have guessed by now (the smart person that you are, as evidenced by your purchase of this book), the drive didn't turn out to be the shortcut I was hoping for. I spent the next ten hours enduring the sharpest curves and steepest mountain grades that Arizona has to offer. When I finally pulled into Flagstaff at 7:30 the next morning, I felt like a frazzled mouse living in a gyroscope operated by a sadistic scientist who was testing its tolerance to vertigo.

I certainly missed the "big picture" because I didn't have an accurate, overall plan or outline for the trip. It would have been simple to check the map key to see what a single red line meant or to have trusted the experts at the Auto Club, who had decades of experience helping plan such trips. Determination to make one's own way without the proper preparation, guideposts, or a reasonable general scheme can be very destructive. You *must* have a plan to succeed, from beginning to end, with the finish line always in sight.

The practical applications of this principle are myriad and apply in almost every situation in which the understanding of principles and concepts is necessary. Even in a romantic situation, it is advantageous to ask the other person for a date—and have them accept—before splurging on floor-seat concert tickets, making dinner reservations, or buying an expensive new outfit. For without the "big picture," which in this case is the date, you really have nothing at all.

BRIGHT MINDS: GET THE "BIG PICTURE" OF BRAIN HEALTH

The concept of the "big picture" applies to more than just your classwork. It also relates to your overall brain health, since that is the foundation that will help you succeed in school. I use the mnemonic BRIGHT MINDS to identify the major factors that either help you perform at a high level or sabotage your schoolwork. When you optimize the following BRIGHT MINDS factors, you change your brain for the better and improve your ability to do your best.

B is for Blood Flow: Healthy blood flow is critical for a high-performing brain. Our brain SPECT imaging shows that low blood flow is associated with ADHD, depression, suicidal thoughts, substance abuse, bipolar disorder, schizophrenia, traumatic brain injury, and more—all of which make it harder to stay motivated and focused on your schoolwork.

Optimization strategies: Engage in physical exercise, practice meditation and/or prayer, and take omega-3 fatty acids and ginkgo biloba.

R is for Rational Thinking: Your thoughts are powerful and can be positive and helpful or, if undisciplined, can be negative and hurtful. I call these damaging thoughts ANTs (automatic negative thoughts).

Optimization strategies: Learn to kill the ANTs that make you feel bad (see chapter 14 for more details).

I is for Inflammation: High levels of inflammation have been associated with decreased motivation,[1] depression, bipolar disorder, OCD, schizophrenia, personality disorders, and more.[2,3] It's also linked with leaky gut, a condition that causes gastrointestinal issues, allergies, and more things that can get in the way of your efforts at school.

Optimization strategies: Eat more foods high in omega-3 fatty acids, reduce intake of foods high in omega-6 fatty acids, and increase prebiotics and probiotics (see chapter 15). Be careful with antibiotics and be sure to floss every day. Have your doctor test your C-reactive protein (CRP) levels, a blood marker for inflammation, as well your omega-3 index (low levels of omega-3 are associated with inflammation).

G is for Genetics: Having family members with brain health/mental health challenges—ADHD, depression, anxiety, addiction, and more—can make you more vulnerable to them. But your genes are not your destiny. Your everyday habits can help turn those bad genes on *or* off.

Optimization strategies: Adopt brain-healthy habits to reduce the impact of genetic vulnerabilities.

H is for Head Trauma: Concussions and head injuries, even if you didn't pass out, can cause lasting issues, including learning problems,[4] ADHD,[5] depression,[6] anxiety and panic disorders,[7] drug and alcohol abuse,[8] and more.

Optimization strategies: Protect your brain. Don't hit soccer balls with your head, and wear a helmet when you ride a bike or go skiing. If you had a head injury, seek treatment—such as hyperbaric oxygen therapy (HBOT) and neurofeedback—to help heal your brain.

T is for Toxins: Environmental toxins found in alcohol, marijuana and cigarette smoke, nonorganic produce, many personal care products, mold, and other everyday items can harm your brain. Exposure to toxins has been associated with learning problems, memory difficulties, brain fog, ADHD, depression, suicide, autism, and more.

Optimization strategies: As much as possible, eliminate toxins from your life. Support your organs of detoxification—the liver, kidneys, and skin—which help flush toxic substances from the body. Your gut also plays a role in detoxification. To support your detoxification system, drink more water (kidneys), reduce alcohol intake (liver), work up a sweat (skin), and eat more fiber (gut).

M is for Mental Health: When you have mental health problems, it makes it much harder to do your best in school. Depression can leave you feeling unmotivated. ADHD can make it hard to focus. Anxiety can mess with your mind on exam days.

Optimization strategies: Address all the BRIGHT MINDS factors and if you're still suffering, seek treatment.

I is for Immunity/Infections: When your immune system is out of whack, it can lead to allergies, infections, autoimmune disease, and even cancer. All of these can get in the way of performing your best at school.

Optimization strategies: Balance your vitamin D levels, avoid allergens, practice stress-management techniques, and get screened for common infections.

N is for Neurohormones: Hormonal imbalances can impact your mind—and your schoolwork—in negative ways. Thyroid abnormalities can sap energy levels and lead to fuzzy thinking, difficulty concentrating, and attention problems. Excess cortisol can make you vulnerable to stress and anxiety. Problems with reproductive hormones can drain motivation and cause mood swings and brain fog.

Optimization strategies: Get your hormone levels checked. Steer clear of "hormone disruptors"—pesticides, certain personal care products and cosmetics—that negatively affect hormone function and production.

D is for Diabesity: Having high blood sugar levels and/or being overweight or obese is known as "diabesity." High blood sugar has been linked to lower blood flow in the brain and a smaller hippocampus, the brain region linked with learning, memory, and moods. Obesity and being overweight are detrimental to brain health and are associated with a smaller brain, decreased blood flow, ADHD, and many other issues.

Optimization strategies: Know your numbers—body mass index (BMI), waist-to-hip ratio, A1C, fasting blood sugar, and fasting insulin levels. Limit pizza and beer (they are not brain foods) and focus your diet on brain-healthy nutrition (see chapter 15).

S is for Sleep: As you sleep, your brain consolidates learning and memory, prepares for the following day, and takes out the neural trash—the cellular debris and toxins that build up during the day.

Optimization strategies: Aim for 7 to 8 hours of sleep a night and follow a healthy sleep regimen. Turn off your tech gadgets at night so they don't interrupt your sleep.

Tap into the power of outlines. In writing, the "big picture" means having an outline of your thoughts before you begin. Such a road map makes it possible to know where you are going. It makes writing an essay or term paper much easier and less time consuming. Diving into writing an essay without an outline means you will probably veer off on tangents, fail to make a cohesive argument, or have to rewrite several times to rearrange passages.

Similarly, in public speaking, it is essential to know where you want to take your audience. It is certainly much simpler to start with general ideas and integrate specifics rather than to begin with isolated details and try to connect them in a logical form.

Keep the context in mind. An idea is easier to understand if you know its context. For example, look at some instances in the development of personality. If you objectively view the behavior of 4-year-olds, you might imagine that they have many psychotic traits. They are frequently found talking to themselves or their invisible friends. They have delusions of grandeur, thinking that they are fictitious characters that they see on television or in books. They also think they can run the house and marry mommy if only daddy will go away! These 4-year-olds seem to be constantly hallucinating, screaming that bears are in their bathrooms or that incredibly large creatures, monsters, whatchamacallits, or whatever are under their beds. If this information on 4-year-olds was not viewed in relation to the "big picture" of their development, our state mental hospitals would look like nursery schools. If you look at all the details or traits put together in the big picture and watch it grow over time, it all begins to make sense. The same goes for studying. Putting the facts you're learning into context helps you grasp their meaning.

Develop a system. In medical school, you will continue running into trees if you do not see the forest. First-year medical students must learn 25,000 new words, and in the second year an additional 25,000 words. If they do not have a system of learning new words and putting them into "the big picture," their brains will undoubtedly go on strike and refuse to process anything but confusion and scattered thoughts. However, if they learn the suffixes, prefixes, and common denominators of root words, the task becomes tolerable.

Develop a system for every subject you learn, whether it's algebra, history, or geography. Once you have a system in place, it simplifies the learning process. It allows you to focus on the material rather than trying to figure out *how* to learn it at the same time.

Put things into historical perspective. If you want to avoid getting discouraged by all the details, it's also important to know where you have been and where you are going. If you feel lost in the details, just stop, seek out the most common idea, then work your way down to the specifics. For example, if you're studying American history and need to know specifics about the ratification of the 19th Amendment to the U.S. Constitution in 1920, your task will be made simpler if you first understand the events of major importance that led up to the event, such as the women's suffrage movement and the efforts of people like Susan B. Anthony and Elizabeth Cady Stanton. If you try to focus on all the micro-details without that main perspective, your brain will become overloaded and will not be able to take in any more information. But if you mentally highlight key points and then break them down from there, you will be much better off.

Favor the "big picture" over the facts. It has been estimated that we remember only 10 to 15 percent of what we learn in high school and college, and that we use less than half of that. Unfortunately, medical school is the same way. (What our patients don't know might hurt them!) Doctors forget many of the facts they once knew; however, understanding the big picture is more important. For example, is it more advantageous for a neuroscientist to know the exact number of neurons in the brain or to understand how those neurons function?

Learn how to learn. Cultural anthropologist Margaret Mead once said, "Children must be taught how to think, not what to think." I think you can replace the word "children" with "students" and her statement is equally true. This same concept arose in a statement that the dean of my medical school gave to my class: "In 10 years, 80 percent of what you learned in medical school will be obsolete [not a very comforting thought!]. You are here not only to learn certain medical subjects, but more importantly, to learn a lifelong method of learning and problem solving." It has been my experience that having a solid foundation and being constantly aware of the "big picture" is more than half of the battle.

Go from the "big picture" to the small details. This principle continues to operate effectively even as you are pursuing the pickiest of details. I know at this point that many of you are saying to yourselves, "It is nice to want to remember this stuff after graduation, but I'm worried about just getting through next Tuesday. The 'big picture' is fine, but you never had Dr. Wilson, whose test next week will question me on the number of electrons of hydrogen in a milliliter of tsetse fly saliva." Believe me, I have had my share of those teachers who thought that their academic corners were the only important ones. The only way that I could do well in their classes was to go from "big picture" ideas to the small details, trying to make sense of it all along the way.

If you schedule yourself and your study time, you'll have the time to get the "big picture" as well as the picky details. If you start with the details, you'll get bogged down and won't ever have the time to get the "big picture."

There was one particular student in my medical school class who was infamous for having the details without the corresponding concepts. He often bragged about the amount of time he studied and the volume of facts he memorized. But because the "big picture" usually escaped him, he had trouble with many tests. He would get outraged when fellow students who had grasped only the "big picture" did better than he did. I recall one time when his roommate (who was in charge of extracurricular partying) got a 99 percent on a histology laboratory exam after studying for only 2 hours. His own grade, however, was 75 percent after studying for more than 10 hours. When he heard the test scores as we were working in the anatomy lab, he fell to his knees and cried out to God over the injustice of it all!

I agree, if you're going to spend the time, you should be rewarded for your effort, but only if you get the "big picture." And remember to study smarter, not harder. If you spend 10 hours focused on the tiny details but don't know where they stem from or how they all connect, that's a waste of time that you could have used for a much-needed break.

CHANGE YOUR BRAIN, CHANGE YOUR GRADES: FROM GENERALIZATIONS TO SPECIFICS

- Start with generalities, then work toward specifics.
- Keep the "big picture" of what you are doing constantly in front of you.
- The "big picture" is what you will remember, and it is your key to understanding the details.

6

GET ORGANIZED

ORGANIZING YOUR CLASSES, YOUR TIME, AND YOURSELF

What do Post-It Notes, the microwave oven, super glue, and Teflon all have in common? They were all invented by accident. If you can come up with a winning invention by chance, you may wonder why you need to be organized or why you need to have a lot of discipline. Take it from Bruno Mars: The world-famous, platinum-selling musical artist says, "You can't knock on opportunity's door and not be ready."

Look at Sir Alexander Fleming, for example. Most people think that when he discovered penicillin in 1928 at St. Mary's Hospital in London, it was a freak accident. It is true that by chance he noticed a mold contaminant on a culture plate of staphylococci, which had resulted in a killing zone of the bacteria. But without his previous foundation in microbiology, the organization of his laboratory, his time, and his discipline to follow through on his discovery, that chance accident might have gone unnoticed for 50 more years. In actual fact, that accident of nature must have occurred many times before, but no one was sufficiently prepared to discover it!

THE CEREBELLUM: THE ORGANIZATION HELPER

Getting organized requires a healthy brain, and especially a healthy cerebellum (and PFC). Latin for "little brain," the cerebellum is located at the back bottom part of the brain, and it plays an essential role in thought coordination, processing complex information, and organization. The cerebellum makes up only 10 percent of the brain's volume, but this powerhouse region is where half of all the brain's neurons reside. Research indicates that the "little brain" is also involved in processing speed, which simply refers to how quickly you can assimilate new information. When activity in the cerebellum is low, people tend to process information more slowly and be more disorganized in their thinking. If your thinking is disorganized, it's going to be hard to organize your studies. Some forms of ADHD (we have identified seven types of ADHD) are related to low activity in the cerebellum, and disorganization is one of the hallmarks of the condition. However, be aware that being somewhat disorganized does *not* mean you have ADHD.

In our brain imaging studies, we also do a series of scans that show brain activity. The white in the following image shows the areas of increased activity. In a healthy scan the cerebellum at the back of the brain is typically the most active.

Cerebellum optimization strategies: Engage in coordination activities, such as table tennis (my favorite), any form of dancing where you need to memorize choreography, yoga, and tai chi. As little as 10 minutes of table tennis boosts activity in the cerebellum (and PFC), according to a Japanese brain imaging study. Go easy with beer and other alcoholic beverages, as alcohol lowers blood flow to the cerebellum, which slows your thinking.

Healthy Active SPECT Scan

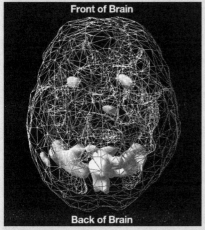

Low Overall Activity

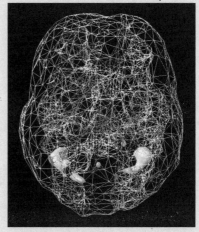

White equals the most active
part of the brain, typically in
cerebellum in back, bottom area

Low activity in the cerebellum

ORGANIZATION PRINCIPLE #1:
SCHEDULE YOUR TIME

So how do you begin putting together an organizational structure that will increase your effectiveness and reduce your study time? First, you need to organize the time you have. Time can be a trusted ally or, as is often the case, a harassing enemy!

Track your time. Before you can organize your time, you need to have an idea of how you spend your 1,440 minutes a day. The best way to do that is to take stock of what you do and how much time you spend doing it. Tracking your daily activities for a full week will give you interesting information about yourself that can be of great value. We often think "I don't have enough time," but in reality, we do have the time, we just have to better allocate the time we have.

Schedule your study time. Now that you've determined how you're currently spending your time, you can decide how to use that time to your advantage. There's an old adage that says you should spend two hours studying for every hour of class time, but as you have probably noticed, this is seldom achieved. Besides, every class is unique, and the amount of study time required will vary with each section of each course you study. The time spent on each subject will also vary with the school that you attend and the grade you're in. If you're in middle school, you don't need to put in as many hours as someone in medical school or law school.

TECH TIP FROM CHLOE AND ALIZÉ
Download a productivity app and use it to track how much time you spend on your homework versus on social media, and use a Fitbit or other tech tools to track your sleeping, eating, class time, work hours, sports activities, and leisure time.

Budget time for all of your courses. First, you need to eyeball your schedule and estimate how much time is required for each class so you can establish a schedule that allows ample time for each subject. Don't neglect the classes outside of your major or those that have fewer units. I remember my first semester of medical school, when gross anatomy was the major hurdle; I was so taken up with anatomy that I neglected a smaller course in histology. I did great in anatomy, but that was at the price of a mediocre grade in histology.

Be realistic. If you are accustomed to spending 20 hours a week studying, setting up a 35-hour-a-week schedule is only inviting disaster! Set yourself up to succeed and make it realistic. If you make it impossible to achieve your goals, you're less likely to be motivated in general. The best way to break old habits and patterns is to give yourself positive, reinforcing experiences. If you lock yourself into an impossible schedule, you will be quickly frustrated and give up the idea altogether. If, however, your schedule is reasonable, then you will find that you can adhere to it, and it will boost your self-esteem! That alone will often motivate you to study better and learn more.

Build in some wiggle room. When creating your schedule, allow for some flexibility. Realize that the first schedule you set up is only a rough estimate of your time, and that it will need to be revised. This revision should take place at least every two weeks and will depend on the difficulty of certain sections in subjects, the dates that term papers are due, the dates of quizzes and mid-terms, and so on.

A time schedule is a lot like a budget. If you're reasonable and flexible in setting it up, then the budget can be of enormous value and security to you, giving you helpful guidelines for spending your money (time) wisely. If, however, you're unreasonable or too rigid with the budget you set up, you will be frustrated by the whole process and toss it to the wind. And you'll feel worse than when you started for failing to follow through with something you began.

ORGANIZATION PRINCIPLE #2: CREATE A PLAN OF ATTACK

The second principle in building your organizational structure is to have a systematic approach for each class that you take.

Lean on your professor. One of the best resources you have is the professor who is teaching the course. Students often think that teachers are too busy for them, or that they don't want to be bothered with questions outside of class. Nothing could be further from the truth. Sure, there are some self-aggrandizing types who think their own research projects are more important than their students, but they are usually the exception. It has been my experience that although most teachers are busy, they welcome personal contact with students, and they derive tremendous satisfaction from showing students how to learn their discipline. Teachers are also often impressed by a student's interest in their class, and that may be an important point if your grade teeters on the borderline between an A and a B or a B and a C.

TECH TIP FROM CHLOE AND ALIZÉ

Check out online reviews of college courses and instructors to find out what to expect from a class.

Don't hesitate to approach the prof and take advantage of their experience and advice on how you should organize yourself for the class. After all, professors have spent six to eight years getting advanced degrees in a particular subject and have likely been teaching it for several years, so they are qualified to guide you through their forest.

Read the syllabus. It is definitely worth your time to read through the syllabus before you

TECH TIP FROM CHLOE AND ALIZÉ
Look for summaries of your required reading online. These aren't meant to replace reading the actual textbook, but they can help you get the "big picture" before tackling the whole book.

actually start the class. Many students never take the time to read the syllabus at any time during a course, let alone before it begins. This is a shame because this document serves several purposes. First, the syllabus is the professor's way of introducing you to what lies ahead for you in the course and what is expected from you, so it will help you know how to schedule your time. Second, it usually gives you the "big picture" right off the bat so you can start the semester with a basic understanding of what's important about the subject. Third, it gives you time to find another class if you realize this one was not what you had in mind.

Get a second (or third or fourth) opinion. If you're unsure about a class, try to find people who have previously taken it from the same instructor and ask them what to expect. Hearing that others have made it out alive and well will make it seem doable. Plus, you'll have a valuable source of advice and information. Ask them:

- how they approached the class
- what was expected from them in class
- what kind of exams were given and how they were graded
- if there were any pop quizzes
- if they have copies of old exams (if the professor does not object, get these!)

- what were the best ways to approach the instructor
- what books were the most useful for the class
- what they liked best or didn't like about the class

If you can, talk to someone who excelled in the class as well as someone who struggled. Sometimes, a student who didn't do well in a class is better able to offer insights into potential challenges you might face, such as an instructor who talks so fast it's impossible to keep up with your notes. If you don't have access to someone who has had the same instructor for a class, it is still helpful to talk to someone who has taken the same class from another professor. They will also have valuable information to share. Do not neglect this gold mine of knowledge!

Check out the textbooks. The required reading list for a class can be an important source of information for organizing your time. As I mentioned above, ask other students which books are valuable for the class and if there are any books on the reading list that are not worth purchasing. In college especially, some professors don't have the "big picture"—or your bank balance—in mind when they choose textbooks. There may be more valuable sources available to you, so look for them. We will explore this important point at length in the next chapter.

Organize your notes. Organizing your notes efficiently can truly have lasting value, and we will explore this topic in depth in chapter 8. But for now, let me just bring up one pertinent point: If you don't organize and file your notes, papers, and exams after you have finished with them, they are almost certainly lost to you! What would you do if, at the end of a long year, you looked at an eight-foot-high stack of old class notebooks piled in the corner? Would you spend hours separating, organizing,

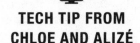

TECH TIP FROM CHLOE AND ALIZÉ

If a teacher speaks too fast to take notes efficiently, record lectures on your smartphone and use voice transcription to create a first draft of notes. Be sure to go through the transcription to correct any mistakes.

and filing them individually? Probably not. If you're like most of us, you would toss the notebooks into the trash.

Luckily for you, computers have made it much easier to organize your notes. If you prefer to take notes on your computer, it helps to keep a separate folder for each class. Organizing all your notes by chapter or unit makes it convenient to study for tests. And it's easy to keep these files for future reference. Believe me, I have gone back to my old notes and papers many times. You may spend up to 30 minutes a week labeling and filing your material, but it is time well spent because you will have something of lasting value. Remember to include time for organizing your notes in your weekly schedule.

ORGANIZATION PRINCIPLE #3: ORGANIZE YOURSELF

The final overarching organization principle relates to you. I touched on discipline earlier in this chapter, and I firmly believe that discipline is the key to organization. Having a disciplined and organized mind will help you accomplish the goals you set for yourself. Dr. M. Scott Peck, the author of *The Road Less Traveled*,[1] says that developing self-discipline involves learning four basic techniques:

- *Learning how to delay gratification,* "which is a process of scheduling the pain and pleasure of life in such a way as to enhance the pleasure by meeting and experiencing the pain first and getting it over with. It is the only decent way to live." This means do your homework first, then check your social media feeds or meet up with your friends in person.
- *Learning to assume responsibility,* which is realizing that you are in charge of your life and your education. Your success as a student is *your* responsibility, not some whim of chance or the fault of poor teachers. The outcome is up to you.

- *Learning to be dedicated to truth and reality.* The truth is that you have sufficient resources, and the reality is that it takes hard work and often long hours to prepare yourself for your goals.
- *Learning the art of balancing,* which Peck says is the discipline that gives us flexibility and is certainly necessary if you want to develop wholeness in your life.

When your mind is organized and disciplined, you will find it much easier to keep your schedule and schoolwork organized.

CHANGE YOUR BRAIN, CHANGE YOUR GRADES: GETTING ORGANIZED

- Discipline and organization are the basic tools required to learn faster and solve problems at school and in life in general.
- Organize your study time by first taking inventory of your available time.
- Set up a realistic and flexible study schedule by estimating how much study time you need for each class and revising the schedule as your needs change.
- Establish a systematic approach to each class by consulting with your professors and with students who have taken the class previously.
- Utilize the syllabus and textbooks in your study approach.
- Organize your notes to get lasting value from them.
- Organize yourself by learning to delay gratification, to assume responsibility, to be dedicated to truth and reality, and to put balance into your life.

7

METHODS TO SUCCESS

METHODS OF STUDY

S tudy methods can either work to your advantage and help you reach your goals faster with less effort, or they can work against you and make it harder for you to achieve success. If your approach to thinking and studying is consistent and leads to rational conclusions and assimilated material, then you have a beneficial method. If, however, your methods of thinking and studying are haphazard or too rigid, you may find yourself in a very unproductive and frustrating state of mind. The most successful students use study methods that are productive and economical, while underachieving students tend to have methods that are frustrating and inefficient.

Everyone has methods for studying; the trick is to develop an effective, systematic approach to learning that works for you. This chapter will introduce you to a variety of study methods. It's up to you to choose the ones that work best for you.

HAVE A GAME PLAN

Creating an overall game plan for your classes involves deciding how you're going to approach each subject *before* the semester begins. One of the best game plans is to "blow out" (not blow off!) the first few weeks of the semester. This means putting maximum effort into doing well in

THE MOST EFFECTIVE METHOD: HARNESS THE POWER OF YOUR PREFRONTAL CORTEX (PFC)

The PFC, which is located behind your forehead, is involved in executive functions, such as planning, focus, forethought, judgment, and organization. It is considered the most human part of the brain and makes up about 30 percent of its total volume. When the PFC isn't working right, it makes it hard for you to come up with an effective study plan and stick with it. Emma came to see me when she was 19 years old because she had just gotten kicked out of college, and she was feeling depressed and anxious about her future. Emma had an IQ of 140, but she was so disorganized and scattered in her approach to schoolwork that she was always turning in assignments late and pulling all-nighters before tests because she hadn't scheduled her time appropriately.

When we scanned Emma's brain while she was resting, her PFC activity looked healthy. But when we scanned her brain while she was focusing on a concentration task, the activity in her PFC *decreased*. In a healthy brain, PFC activity should increase when concentrating. A decrease in PFC activity is a classic sign of ADHD, and with a comprehensive treatment plan, Emma was able to reenroll in college. She got organized, came up with a study plan, stuck with it, and graduated with honors.

If you struggle with organization and planning or with inattention and restlessness—even if you don't have ADHD—it's important to strengthen your PFC. Boosting dopamine is the key. (See chapter 2 for specific ways to enhance the function of the PFC.)

the first part of your classes. Many students think they can ease into the new school year and spend the beginning of the semester catching up on partying with friends they haven't seen all summer. This is a big mistake. Blowing off this part of the year is dangerous. It leaves you behind in classes, and you often miss important foundational material. Not only that, but the first week or so leaves an impression for the rest of the year not only on your teachers and peers but also on yourself. If you're prepared and work hard at the start of the year, you're more likely to continue that way, and it will be much easier to stay on track.

If you follow the principle of doing well in the beginning, you will notice at least three positive effects on the rest of your semester:

- First, your effort will be on establishing a solid foundation, and as we have seen before, building knowledge on a good foundation is a lot easier than building on one made of sand.
- Second, by working hard during the first part of the semester, you will do well in the class and subsequently build your self-esteem. With your confidence improved, it will be easier for you to continue in a positive and productive way. You will feel good about yourself because your efforts will have paid off. This is a lot easier to do in the beginning because the material is usually foundational. If you are missing that foundation, you will find that your efforts are not paying high dividends, thus decreasing your stimulus to put forth the effort.
- Third, if you do well in the beginning, you will leave yourself some breathing room in the event of a disruption in your personal life making it difficult for you to study for a week or two. This could be something negative, such as illness, or positive, such as meeting someone special who makes it hard to concentrate on anything else. You will also do better in your classes simply because you will be under less pressure to perform.

This foundational principle is one of the chief reasons for my success in college and medical school. By obtaining a solid foundation, developing self-confidence, being rewarded for my effort, and leaving myself breathing room to learn under less pressure, I was able to achieve my immediate academic goals.

AVOID THE TEST-TO-TEST SYNDROME

Another aspect of the game plan involves learning how not to spend the semester simply going from test to test. This a common syndrome in college and is almost the norm in medical school. Many students survive in school by studying for only one test at a time—the next one—and leaving all other work until after the exam. But as my own work with students will verify, there is a price to pay for this habit in the form of anxiety, high blood pressure, and insomnia.

Schedule your time, not just during a study session, but throughout the semester (see chapter 6 for tips). If you adhere to a reasonable schedule, you can eliminate, or at least decrease, the test-to-test syndrome as a study method. This will give you a more positive outlook and a healthier body.

GO BEYOND YOUR TEXTBOOKS

If you're like many students, you may believe your education begins and ends with the first and last pages of your textbooks. You may not realize that there are many other materials that can be even more valuable than those textbooks. Specifically, I am referring to three sources: review books, recent journal or online articles, and old exams.

Use review or outline books. I call these "big picture" books because they give you the straight stuff you need to remember. These resources are great for getting a quick overview before you read your text and are also very useful for review later. If you happen to come across some useful information, highlight it or write it on a sticky note and attach it to the rest of your study materials. Do not, however, use them as your only source. If you do, you will likely find that the facts will not make as much sense as they should. You can find out about these books from your teachers or fellow students or by going to the library or by searching an online bookstore. Scour the internet for additional articles and resources, but make sure they are reliable sources—and sorry, but note that Wikipedia itself is *not* a reliable source, although the sources listed at the end of a Wikipedia entry may prove to be useful.

Read recent journal and online articles. If you train yourself in school to be informed on the latest developments in your field of interest, you will carry this trait with you into your professional life. Periodical literature, besides giving you the most current information, often will present a topic more clearly and concisely than your textbook. Find the online journals that are most beneficial to your studies and use the information in them to your advantage.

Review old exams. Get your hands on some old exams—*if your professor doesn't mind!* Be aware that some professors frown on this and some categorically refuse to hand out old tests, while others see no problem with it. Old tests can be as valuable a resource as your textbook, lecture notes, or review books. They will show you what the professor thinks is important to learn, thus guiding your study. They will illustrate how the professor writes test questions so you can determine how to answer the questions. Also, studying old exams is an excellent review method for testing yourself on the material. Finally, teachers have a difficult time making up new test questions each year, so questions on old tests will likely reappear on the current test. Be smart and try to get copies of old tests from previous students or from the professor. You can easily make flash cards based on the old test questions and study them on your phone or carry them with you.

TECH TIP FROM CHLOE AND ALIZÉ
Quizlet is a great app you can use to create flashcards.

LEARN THE PRELUDES TO METHODS

Before I discuss the different methods of study, I want to mention a few simple statements or principles that I believe are basic to all good study methods.

Do a quick recap. Before beginning a study session, quickly review the material you studied the day before. This will increase your exposure to it and will also give you an opportunity to test your understanding and recall of it.

TECH TIP FROM CHLOE AND ALIZÉ
Use the timer on your smartphone to let you know when it's time to move on to the next study unit.

Study in units that are defined. Before a study session, carefully and systematically choose a block of material to be covered. In this way, you'll have specific goals for your time and can regulate the amount of material you cover. Divide all of your study material by the amount of time you have to study, so you know how much time to devote to each section. This way, each time you complete a section, you'll feel like you're making progress, and it won't seem like endless work.

Rewrite for better comprehension. If you're having trouble with a statement that is poorly written, try to rephrase it in your own words. If you do this, your retention of the point will be especially increased.

Make sure you understand the material. Memorizing material doesn't necessarily mean you have actually learned it. Learning follows understanding. If you understand what you have memorized, then you have learned the material. On the other hand, if you can recite facts but cannot make sense of them, you may pass the test, but you haven't learned anything.

Apply what you learn. At every opportunity available to you, try to take what you have learned and make a practical application of it. Make connections between everyday activities and the material. This way, when you're taking a test, you'll remember that situation. Application is integral to retention.

Shore up your foundation. If you're having problems in the beginning of a class, go back to the basics. It's better to strengthen your foundation than to waste a semester in confusion.

5 SUREFIRE STUDY METHODS FOR SUCCESS

I recommend five specific study methods to increase your chances of success:

1. Preview/review. Previewing and reviewing will tells you where you are going and where you have been—two-thirds of the work.

Getting an overview before you dive into a subject and summarizing what you have learned are the two principles that frame the "big picture." If you practice reading the summaries and skimming the material as you begin, you'll know what to expect during your study session, and you'll be able to develop a plan for completing your task.

Then, as your study session is nearing its conclusion, take a few minutes to write a short summary of what you have learned. This practice will reinforce your understanding and will provide insight into particular problem areas.

2. Test making. One of my favorite study methods is making up test questions during and after the study period. By doing this, you learn to pick out the important facts and reinforce what you have studied. If you write these questions, you will have a good, quick source of review to consult right before an exam. When I studied, I kept a separate piece of paper with my own questions on it (with the answers on the back). It often turned out that I would have 30 to 50 percent of the test on those sheets of paper.

If you have questions on the material you are studying, you should also make notes of these and seek clarification from the professor or other sources. Keeping a record of questions about the material you do not understand is helpful in review, because if you had trouble with the material initially, you will likely need more review to master it.

Creating your own test questions on the material you do not understand will take time and will slow you down initially. However, this practice will save you time and energy in the long run because you won't need to read through the textbook or your notes four or five times before you assimilate the material.

3. Underlining. Underlining (or highlighting) important material in textbooks or notes is a very popular method of study and, if used properly, it can be a valuable tool in your study arsenal. However, this method is often overdone. There was a student in my medical school class who underlined virtually everything in his text or notes—using 14 different colors to denote the degree of importance for the material! Underlining while you study is effective for three reasons:

- First, it helps you focus on what's important. If you underline everything, you're wasting your time. Select the summary sentence of a paragraph, the main fact statements, and important supporting material. Underline what you want to remember and what you think might be on exams.
- Second, underlining helps you be active. By selecting important statements to underline, you are forcing yourself to take an active role in studying, so you will be less likely to passively read through the material and miss important points. You will instead be interacting with it.
- Third, underlining helps you review. If you have the pertinent points highlighted, then you can quickly review what you have studied. If you have underlined nothing (or everything), you will have to waste time plodding through all of it to review.

4. Outlining. If it is done concisely and thoughtfully, outlining will re-expose you to the material in a slower, more methodical manner, thus increasing the chance for retention. In addition, as with underlining, you'll be taking an active role in your studies by deciding what information is important enough to rewrite. It is easy to underline everything in a book, but when you outline, you'll force yourself to restate only the important material. And finally, outlining provides you with a valuable tool for review when it is time to study for the test. Many students, even after they have underlined their texts, never go back to their books before the exam. They instead rely on their notes and outlines.

Outlining is simple. Start by putting the textbook title, lecture title, or major topic at the top of the page. Below that, list the main concepts covered. Label each one with Roman numerals (I, II, III, IV, V). Under those, use numbers or just bullet points to list the most important things you need to remember.

However, there are disadvantages to outlining. First, this method can be very time-consuming, and if you are very busy, you'll have trouble doing it consistently. Second, outlining demands a patient individual who can see the value of slowly going through new material. If you're the type who wants to study as quickly as possible, outlining may not be for you.

If you decide to create outlines, highlight the important facts of new material in a consistent fashion.

5: Pretend to be a teacher. Imagine that you're teaching a class and have to present the information you've learned in your own words. Explain the concepts out loud as if you were in front of a room full of students. This is one of the best ways to pinpoint the material you've understood and reveal the concepts that need additional review.

In conclusion, realize that you are unique. After you have given each method a fair trial, choose the ones that work best for you.

CHANGE YOUR BRAIN, CHANGE YOUR GRADES: METHODS TO STUDY

- Do your best in the first part of the semester. This will help you establish a solid foundation, build your self-esteem, and leave you some breathing room.
- Take advantage of "other" materials, including review books, online magazine articles, and old exams. There is more to education than the textbooks.
- Make the "preludes to methods" part of your study symphony. These include beginning study sessions with a quick review of previous work, studying in defined units, rewording poorly written statements, learning by first understanding, and applying what you learn.
- Use overview and summary techniques.
- Create test questions for yourself to check your comprehension and to learn how to choose important facts.
- Underline to focus, to be active, and to review.
- Create outlines only if you're a patient person since it is time consuming.
- Pretend to be a teacher to gauge how well you've understood the material.

8

IT'S A CLASS ACT

CLASS SKILLS

Screaming 5-year-olds clutch their mommy's leg and look as though Godzilla is waiting for them behind the classroom door. Then they plead with their mommy, asking, "Why do I have to go to kindergarten?" Years later, those same students have given up the screaming and leg clutching, but they may still be asking the same question: "Why do I have to go to class?" Their rationalization skills have likely improved. They leave Godzilla out of the argument and contend that they can get all the necessary information online or that their classes are so boring that someone could get rich by recording them and selling the lectures to incurable insomniacs.

If you can relate to these thoughts and think going to class is a big waste of time, it may simply be because you're lacking in some basic class skills. When you have the skills needed to operate at peak efficiency during class, you can greatly reduce your study time and perform better on homework and exams.

Before I discuss the specific skills necessary for making class time a successful experience, I first want to answer the question, "Why should I go to class?" There are many reasons for attending class:

- increase your knowledge of a particular subject
- have the professor clarify questionable points for you
- meet other students

- observe how other students approach the class
- find a compatible study partner
- make sure you aren't dropped from the roster (if attendance is required)

Of course, the most important reason to attend class is the lecture itself. During the lecture, you will usually be taught:

- how to learn the subject
- what information the teacher thinks is important
- what will be on exams (important clues for exams are almost always given in class)
- how to assimilate the subject so it will have practical value for you

If you master the lecture, your study time will decrease significantly because you'll know what is important and how to go about learning and assimilating it. In this chapter, you'll discover seven strategies that will help you get the most out of class time.

THE MINDFULNESS EQUATION: BEING PRESENT IN THE MOMENT ADDS UP TO MORE GRAY MATTER

You may have heard about the power of mindfulness to help you calm stress and relax, but did you know it can help your brain? Research shows that mindfulness meditation increases the brain's gray matter volume in brain regions involved in learning and memory processes, self-regulation, and more.[1] Basically, mindfulness is intentionally focusing your attention on something. For the purposes of making the most of the classroom experience, being mindful means being fully present and paying attention in class.

1. BE PREPARED

Once you've made the commitment to attend class faithfully, the next important step is to prepare yourself for what is going to happen there. As I said earlier, preparation is paramount to accomplishment.

Prepare yourself. This means you need to get enough sleep the night before. Did you know that getting less than six hours of sleep at night is associated with lower overall brain activity and can adversely affect your productivity? Aim for seven to eight hours of sleep each night. You also need to eat in the morning before school and at lunchtime to maintain your mental energy, but don't eat too much or it can make you fall asleep. (You'll discover much more about what to eat to help you stay focused and alert in chapter 15.) Get some physical exercise every day. Regular exercise has been found to improve memory, relieve stress, and boost moods, as well as reduce symptoms of ADHD, depression, and anxiety.

Read the syllabus. It's important to know what is going to be happening in class *before* the class starts. Believe me, it is very disheartening to get to class only to discover that you forgot about the midterm that day or the paper that is due. Read the course outline and find out what is happening.

Read the section of the text that deals with the upcoming class. This serves three purposes. First, it familiarizes you with new vocabulary words, thus decreasing the distraction of asking your friend, "What's a cluster headache? Could it be this class?" While they are laughing at your question, you both have missed the next three important points. A tip is to write down all

---

TECH TIP FROM CHLOE AND ALIZÉ

If you're taking an online course, understand that communication is different from a face-to-face setting. Online classes that are straight lectures can be very beneficial and big time-savers. But if a class involves demonstrations or requires student interaction, you may be better off in a classroom setting.

of your questions as you go and save them for after class so you don't miss anything in between. Second, reading ahead gives you the opportunity to solidify new information, because the lecture will be your second exposure to the material. After reading the text you may have some unanswered questions, which you can then ask in class. Third, you'll be able to participate intelligently in class, which will further solidify the material as well as impress the professor (which is not the goal, but certainly cannot hurt).

2. SET GOALS

Set specific goals for what you want to accomplish during class. Getting a little ahead in whatever material you can will help optimize your time in class and relieve some stress. These goals may involve having your questions answered, seeing what the professor emphasizes in a certain section, and trying to figure out what will be on the exam.

One goal that I always had when preparing for class was to try to get a copy of the professor's lecture notes. This was not always possible, because many teachers lecture from memory or do not want their notes copied. It has been my experience, however, that most teachers have extensive notes on their lecture topic. If they are approached in the right way, they are happy to let students copy them.

The advantages of having these notes are obvious: You won't have to worry that your notes are incomplete, and you'll often find the important points underlined or starred, thus emphasizing what the teacher thinks is important. Even if you do get a copy of your teacher's notes, I still recommend taking notes during class because it is a method of active learning that keeps your brain engaged and reduces your chances of tuning out or daydreaming during class.

3. AVOID DISTRACTIONS AND STAY AWAKE

To get the most out of class, you need to minimize distractions so you can stay focused, and you need to stay awake and alert. The number one rule is to be sure to use the restroom before class. You simply can't concentrate on what the instructor is saying if you're in desperate need of a bathroom break. Similarly, if you feel like you're dying of thirst or your stomach is grumbling loudly, it will be hard to stay focused on the class material. Make it a habit to bring a water bottle with you and carry snacks you can munch on in between classes. Classrooms are often too hot or too cold, so dress in a way that allows you to add or remove a layer to keep comfortable. And try to avoid sitting next to students who talk loudly or use their phones during class, who annoyingly tap their pens on the tabletop, or who eat smelly food during class. Sitting near the front of the class lessens distractions and helps you observe the professor better, thus enabling you to pick up nonverbal cues that would not be as evident from farther away.

Did you know that checking your phone in class could cost you half a grade on exams? That's what researchers at Rutgers University discovered in a 2018 study.[2] The study found that having a tech device in class didn't lower comprehension in that particular lecture, but it reduced scores on final exams by 5 percent, which is the equivalent of half a grade. What's more surprising is that students who *didn't* have a device in class also got lower scores if others in the lecture used their tech tools.

> ⬚
>
> **TECH TIP FROM CHLOE AND ALIZÉ**
> If you can't resist the temptation to scroll through your social media feed or check your messages, put your phone away in your purse or backpack so you can't see it.

If you find that you tend to fall asleep in class, here are a few suggestions that may help. First, try drinking some cold water before class. Did you know that fatigue can be a sign of dehydration? Water makes up more than half your body weight, and your brain and body can't function optimally without it. A glass of water before or during class can help you feel more awake and refreshed. Some students find that fidgeting with a small toy—quietly!—can help keep you stimulated as well. If you keep your hands busy, you'll be less likely to nod off. Of course, don't do this if you need to be taking notes. Another helpful technique to avoid falling asleep during class is to sit as near to the front of the room as possible. It's embarrassing to fall asleep in class, so if you're in direct view of the teacher, you'll be less likely to snooze.

4. UNDERSTAND THAT HEARING DOES NOT EQUAL LISTENING

Many of you may be asking, "Why do I need to read about how to listen? I've been doing it all of my life." I've got news for you: Just because you've been doing something for a long time does not necessarily mean your skill level is enviable. If you take a poll among parents and children, husbands and wives, you will invariably find complaints about nearly everyone's skill in listening.

There are five major steps for effective listening in a classroom situation:

- *Put yourself in a position to adequately hear the lecturer.*
  This means sitting close to the front of the room, keeping
  distractions out of sight, and asking the professor to speak up
  (or repeat) if you're having trouble hearing.
- *Process what you hear.* Hearing, by itself, gives you little or
  no information. Think of all the millions of things you hear
  every day that your brain never processes—street noise, birds
  chirping, other people talking on their phone, your roommate's
  YouTube videos, and so on. You need to pay attention in order
  to process what is being said.
- *Acknowledge that you have heard and processed the information.*
  A classroom situation is a two-way street and should involve
  feedback to the professor as the material is being presented.
  Otherwise, you could just listen to lecture tapes. If the professor
  doesn't think anyone is paying attention to the lecture,
  enthusiasm will diminish and put an end to any chance for

an interesting and stimulating class. We all need feedback, so acknowledge the lecturer with nods when you understand what is being said or with questions when you do not. This is part of being an active listener.

- *React to the lecture.* If you're hearing, processing, and acknowledging what is being presented during a lecture, you will usually react to it on an emotional level. This can be good if you agree with what is being said, because you'll feel an emotional bond with the professor. It can even be good if you disagree with what is being presented, because you can have a dialogue on the subject, thus increasing your knowledge and maybe even increasing the professor's. Remember that if you disagree with the teacher, that doesn't mean you have nothing in common and can't learn from them. Disagreement is valuable, if only to solidify your own stand on a subject. People who don't think like you still have much to offer, so be tolerant and get as much information from your instructor as you can.

- *Assimilate what you've heard.* After you have heard, processed, acknowledged, and reacted to what was presented in class, it's time to make the information a part of yourself. This task can be accomplished only if you have the big picture of the lecture in mind and understand how and why the information is important for the class and your educational goals. If you can take what was said and give practical meaning to it, assimilation is taking place. If you're near the end of a lecture and are having trouble doing this, ask the instructor to help you put it together. Discover the importance of what you are doing and how it all fits into the big picture. It will make you an active listener.

5. BECOME A NOTE-TAKING PRO

In order to be a successful student, you need to learn to be a swift and efficient note-taker. Why is note-taking so important? You may think you have a very good memory, but each semester the average student spends more than 250 hours in lectures, and by the time finals week arrives, those first few weeks of class may seem decades away.

Notes are the best source for reviewing for exams. In my experience, I found that more than 75 percent of the test material for most courses is covered in the lectures. If you take good notes and study them, this usually results in an automatic 75 percent or higher on a test; the rest is icing on the cake. Moreover, if you have a good set of notes, your study time will decrease because you'll have most of the important material in front of you, and you'll have more direction about how to learn it.

TECH TIP FROM CHLOE AND ALIZÉ

If you take notes on your laptop or tablet, be sure to have a file open and ready to go when class begins. Create a folder for each class and use separate files for each lecture named by date so you can find them easily. After class, go through your notes and **bold** or highlight the most important concepts.

Another reason for taking good notes is that you'll then have them when you need to study for any national exams that you might take, such as the ACT or SAT, GRE, MCAT, LSAT, and so on. And as I have learned over and over again, notes can be a valuable reference source for you in years to come.

Taking good notes takes practice. The following tips can help you master the art of note-taking.

Invest in the right tools. Whether you prefer typing on a laptop or handwriting in a spiral notebook, make sure you have the tools that work best for you.

Make your notes readable. If your writing is so tiny you can barely see it or it's illegible, there is no sense in spending the time taking notes. Write as clearly as you can. If a teacher speaks so fast that you're having trouble getting everything down, ask them to slow down. Most instructors will be glad to do so and will welcome the feedback. Chances are if you are having trouble keeping up, so are others.

Label your notes for easy searching. Put the date and the specific subject of the lecture at the top of that day's notes. This will help you organize them when studying for exams and will also help you file them.

Use abbreviations. To take notes faster, use abbreviations. It doesn't matter if you make them up; just be consistent in their usage. Some common ones that I use are:

#	number
@	at
~	about or approximately
b/c	because
b4	before
btwn	between
esp	especially
etc	et cetera, and so on
ex	for example
ie	such as
impt	important
re	regarding
s/t	something
tho	though
w/	with
w/i	within
w/o	without
x	times (e.g., 5x a day)
yrs	years

Organize your lecture notes. Teachers usually follow an outline in lecturing. If you can incorporate their outline into your notes, the notes will be easier to follow and refer to later. If you cannot detect an outline in the lecture, then roughly make your own as you go along.

Leave margins. When taking notes, be sure that you leave yourself plenty of room to fill in gaps that will inevitably occur. It's a good idea to leave a wide margin at the left-hand side of the paper. This will enable you to put main ideas in the margin to indicate what is in the body of the notes.

Delineate lists. If a teacher says they are going to explain five steps of a chemical process, four reasons why the Civil War started, or three types of brain disorders, be sure to make a numbered list of those key elements. You can also use dashes, bullet points, asterisks, or stars to indicate the major points in a list.

TECH TIP FROM CHLOE AND ALIZÉ

If you have trouble making up your own abbreviations for common words that you use a lot, check online for lists of abbreviations.

Compare notes. It's very helpful to have another, trusted person in your class with whom you can compare notes. This practice will help both of you fill in the gaps and check your accuracy.

Write the right amount. I have known students who sit back and try to assimilate the material by just hearing the lecture and jot down only a few words here and there in their notebooks. I have also known students who compulsively write every word that is said. It's obvious that the answer lies somewhere in between these two extremes. If you're having trouble striking a balance, make sure to tip the scale toward the compulsive note-taker's side. Copious notes are worthwhile, and you can eliminate the excess when you review your notes later. The most important clues about how much to write will come from the professor. The more effort it takes to explain the material to you, the more you should take notice of what they are trying to say. The syllabus takes a great deal of effort to prepare, so know what is in it.

Check the board. If a teacher writes anything on the chalkboard or white board—names, dates, tables, charts, terminology—write it in your notes. It takes effort for the professor to do that, so you should recognize the emphasis they are making.

Watch for verbal and nonverbal cues in the lecture. If a teacher says that something is important, why doubt it? After all, the teacher is the one who will be creating the test. If something is repeated in class three different ways, take note of the increased effort on the teacher's part, and be sure that you have that point on paper. If a teacher pauses and looks as if they are waiting for you to write the point, write it. Watch for changes in tone of voice and listen to the emphasis placed on certain words. Also be aware of what the teacher's body language is telling you. Learn to observe and really get to know your instructors. It is a skill to be able to read them, and the only way to become skillful at this is to make a conscious effort to try to put together what they say and how they say it.

Highlight the big stuff. When it becomes obvious that you do not understand a point, put a big question mark next to it in your notes so that you won't forget to go back to it and have it clarified. Likewise, if you know that something is important, underline or star it so that you will remember its importance later. And by all means, if a professor says that something is going to be on a test, make appropriate notation of the fact.

Get the big picture. After the big stuff, it's time to fill in as many details as you and the teacher deem necessary. Remember, take your cues from the lecturer—they are getting paid to do it.

Stick it out 'til the end. The last point I want to make on note-taking involves persevering to the end. The last 10 to 15 minutes of a class are usually very important. The teacher will likely summarize the main points and illustrate their practical usage. They will also tell you what to expect next time. Many students are so impatient for the class to end (constantly looking at the classroom clock, hoping that the lecturer will see them and get the hint) that they miss some important information. Be attentive to the end to get the most out of the class.

6. MASTER THE ART OF ASKING QUESTIONS

Asking questions in class can be a tricky business. On the one hand, you want clarification on any points you've misunderstood. On the other hand, if you ask a long, detailed question with only two minutes left in the class, you risk annoying your classmates who can't wait to rush off to their next class or to lunch. Here are some suggestions to help make your questions count.

Make sure your questions are pertinent. I have heard it said that there is no such thing as a stupid question. If you had attended class with me and heard a particular student ask the sort of questions that even trivia books would think are trivial, you would agree that some questions are indeed stupid, or at least inappropriate. Be sensitive and don't waste your classmates' valuable time. If your question is trivial or goes off on a tangent, that's okay; just ask the professor about it after class. Reserve in-class time for questions that pertain directly to the subject matter.

TECH TIP FROM CHLOE AND ALIZÉ
If you don't get to ask all your questions in class and your teacher isn't available after class, ask for their email address so you can email your questions. Most college professors and some high school teachers give students their contact info so you can ask questions. You can also visit instructors during their office hours for additional assistance.

If you're getting lost, ask sooner rather than later. If you find yourself losing the big picture in class, odds are that other students feel the same way. The sooner you ask the teacher to stop and direct you to it, the better. The teacher will be glad to clarify questionable points up front rather than go back to them later.

Be as specific as possible. If you ask a question in a vague or open-ended way, the professor might not address the piece that's stumping you.

Don't hesitate to challenge your teacher in a respectful manner. If you don't agree with a professor and want them to further defend their position on a subject, that's okay. It's one of the best ways for students and teachers to learn from one another. If the teacher is truly knowledgeable on the subject, they won't be threatened by you. Learning to debate in a mutually respectful manner is a good habit to acquire.

Don't hog class time with your questions. Give others a chance to ask questions and join the dialogue. Also, when it is near the end of the class, consider saving the question until after class. Being polite is also an art!

7. REVIEW THE CLASS

After class is over, what then? For some students, the moment they walk out of class, they forget everything about that subject until the next time they step into the classroom. This is *not* the way to be a successful student. With a little effort outside the classroom, you can ensure better performance on homework, essays, and tests.

Go to the professor and clarify any questionable areas in your notes. The sooner these areas are clearly understood, the better.

Recopy your notes as soon after class as possible. While redoing your notes might seem time-consuming and unproductive, it can serve several important functions. First, the simple act of copying your notes will reinforce the material in your mind and help you retain it better. It is a well-known fact that if you review the material within a short time after class, you will remember it longer than if you don't see it again for two weeks. Second, it allows you to reorganize scattered or rushed notes and make them more orderly and readable. Third, redoing your notes gives you the opportunity to fill in any gaps and answer any questions that you had about them during class time. Finally, a complete set of notes will serve you well when test time draws near, and even beyond that if you end up taking advanced courses in the same area. If you do not buy in to this idea, at least go over your notes within 72 hours for re-exposure and to fill in the gaps.

Make up questions on important information that you think will be on the test. Write these in your new set of notes. If you practice, you can become so good at anticipating what will be on exams that you will have answered a majority of the test in your notes. See how good you are at getting on the professor's wavelength.

Make a companion set of "big picture" fact sheets. These notes contain only major points and can be useful for quick study immediately before an exam. If you write these sheets as you go, they will be of tremendous value to you.

CHANGE YOUR BRAIN, CHANGE YOUR GRADES: CLASS SKILLS

- Go to class to increase knowledge, clarify questions, interact with other students, find a compatible study partner, and keep your attendance record in order.
- Prepare for class by getting adequate sleep, staying hydrated, staving off hunger, sitting close to the front, and realizing that what is said in class is usually on the exams.
- Effective listening in class involves hearing, processing, acknowledging, reacting, and assimilating.
- Lecture notes are usually your best review source for exams.
- When note-taking, use abbreviations, write as clearly as possible, ask the professor to slow down if you're having trouble keeping up, leave plenty of room for the main ideas in the margins, and compare your notes with another student.
- When deciding how much to write, be cognizant of the effort that the teacher has expended to convey the information and watch for verbal and nonverbal cues.
- When asking questions, keep to the point, ask questions as soon as they come up, be specific, and be polite.
- Recopy your notes to improve legibility, reorganize them, fill in the gaps, and re-expose yourself to the material.
- Make up your own test questions, and create "big picture" fact sheets.

9

PARIETAL RELATIONS

Memorize Faster with Better Retention

"**A**rgyle met three fenderless valiants, while Lucy tripped on his lice." *Huh?* I know this sounds like a great beginning to a science fiction novel where the main character, an argyle sock, meets three cars in a bad section of town after their fenders have been ripped off. Meanwhile, the sock's owner, a man named Lucy, is tripping over some very large lice. This kooky picture survives many years after my friend Alan Richardson, MD, coined it to help remember the 10 essential amino acids (protein building blocks). Here's what that strange sentence means:

"Arg/ile (arginine, isoleucine) met (methionine) three (threonine) fenderless (phenylalanine) valiants (valine) while Lucy (leucine) tripped (tryptophan) on his (histidine) lice (lysine)."

This is one of the best examples of how to boost your memory by using a specific region of your brain called the parietal lobe. Located near the back of your head, the parietal lobe is involved in sensory processing and directional sense. It also has very powerful associative properties that make this type of memory technique work. All Alan did was take things that he knew—argyle socks, fenders, lice, and so on—and associate them with new material that he wanted to remember. He stored the information in his brain as he learned it, and those associations provided a way for him to start looking for the material when he needed to retrieve it.

The skill of being able to recall what you have learned is one that has infinite value to students. In this chapter, you'll discover several techniques that will help you develop a better memory so you can learn information faster and retain it longer.

HOW THE BRAIN MAKES MEMORIES

Making memories is a complex process that takes raw input from your senses—sight, hearing, smell, touch, and taste—and converts these experiences into memories. There are three primary steps involved in memory-making:

1. **Encoding** occurs when your brain pays attention to sensory input, whether unconsciously due to emotions tied to the experience (think of your first kiss) or by consciously focusing on something (as in the case of studying). Research indicates that when we associate a purpose with experiences and events, we tend to recall them more clearly and retain them longer.

2. **Storage** occurs when your brain makes it possible for you to retrieve the memories you have encoded. The hippocampi, located in the temporal lobes, act as gateways in the storage process. Contrary to what you may think, memories aren't neatly collected into one central storage unit in the brain for easy retrieval. They are typically broken up into small chunks and tucked away in several areas of the brain.

3. **Recall** is when your brain retrieves an encoded, stored memory. To do so, your brain has to actively search out and gather all those little chunks and put them back together. It isn't as simple as hitting "play" on a video on your smartphone. It's more like one of those TV movies that depict a reenactment of an event. This helps explain why different people's memories of the same event can differ and how memories can evolve over time. Recalling memories stimulates neural pathways, and actively working your memory strengthens it.

Memory and the Seahorse Twins

If you had a million-dollar racehorse, would you feed it junk food? Would you give it beer or put drugs in its food? Of course not! As an intelligent person, you would never treat such a valuable horse that way. Did you know there is an even more valuable horse-shaped structure in your brain? Actually, you have two of them, but if you're like most people, you probably aren't aware of them or their importance. No bigger than your thumbs, they reside within your temporal lobes, which is part of your emotional brain. We call them the hippocampi, which is Greek for "seahorse," because their shape resembles the cute marine creature.

These two structures play a vital role in your memory. They help you remember where you left your history book, the names of the all the important brain regions for your anatomy class, and what you studied last night for today's quiz. You can help keep your hippocampus healthy by optimizing the BRIGHT MINDS factors featured in chapter 5.

MEET THE THREE TYPES OF MEMORY

To begin, let's take a brief look at the three types of memory: immediate, short-term, and long-term.

Immediate Memory. Your immediate memory enables you to remember information for less than a second, just long enough to apply it or respond to it. It allows you to process only one thing at a time. Most of these memories are lost since they are not encoded. Here are a few examples of how you use immediate memory in your schoolwork.

- When you're rewriting a paper, you use your immediate memory every time you transcribe a few words.
- When you're reading a textbook, you continually use your immediate memory to give yourself the chance to process what is printed.
- When you're listening to a lecture, you use your immediate memory to take notes.

The best way to improve your immediate memory capability is to *pay attention* to what you're doing, reading, or listening to. Your immediate memory initially intakes material; you then decide whether to discard the material or to put it into your short-term memory bank.

Short-Term Memory. Your PFC governs short-term memory, allowing you to temporarily store several pieces of information for a short time (a minute or less). The loss of this type of memory is one of the hallmarks of Alzheimer's disease or other forms of dementia. In diagnosing this syndrome, I typically ask the patient to remember three things—for example, a '66 Chevy, a red ball, and Lombard Street in San Francisco. Then I will ask the person to tell me the three things several minutes later. The dementia patient, having an impaired short-term memory, will usually not respond correctly.

Short-term memory is enhanced by concentrating on the information to be retained, understanding the information in its context, and grouping similar pieces of information together. If you find that you're losing the capacity to retain thoughts for a few minutes, try to concentrate on what you're doing, and you should find that your short-term memory will improve. Sometimes just reminding your brain to remember something will actually help you make that connection (ironic, right?).

Short-term memory serves as a transition between immediate and long-term memory. After deciding to retain something, you remember it long enough in your short-term memory to work on its long-term retention.

Long-Term Memory. Long-term memory involves the retention of material beyond a few minutes and could last for days, weeks, or even years. The number of items that can be stored in your long-term memory is limitless. Long-term memories are processed in the hippocampus, then stored in a variety of brain regions—sounds in the temporal lobes, visual cues in the occipital lobes, sensory cues in the parietal lobes, and so on. Undoubtedly, you have subconsciously found many ways to organize and retrieve the information stored here. However, if you systematically order the material you want to remember into associations that your parietal lobe can catalog for you, it will be easier to retrieve.

These three types of memory operate interdependently. In order to deposit information into your long-term memory bank, you must first make substantial deposits into your immediate and short-term memory accounts.

MEMORY IN THE BRAIN

Type of Memory	Length of Time It Lasts	Associated Brain Region
Immediate	Less than 1 second	Visual-sensory cortex (parietal/occipital lobes)
Short-term	Less than 60 seconds	Prefrontal cortex
Long-term	Hours to years	Hippocampus, the brain's "gateway" memory structure

WHY MEMORY FAILS

Before outlining specific techniques for improving your long-term memory, let's first explore four common reasons why memory fails.

A lack of focus on the details. If you don't pay attention to what is being presented, the material will not enter any memory system. It will be lost before there is any chance of assimilation. This is often the reason why we have a hard time remembering names; we simply don't focus on them. Stay away from anything that will divert your attention from your purpose. If you want to remember something important, make a point to stay laser-focused on the information—and I mean I want you to actually picture lasers coming from your brain as in *Star Wars*. Now that's hard to forget!

A lack of understanding of what you are trying to memorize. If you don't comprehend the information you're trying to store, you won't know where to put it in your memory bank. Absentmindedly repeating phrases that you don't understand is a poor way to study and an inefficient use of time.

A lack of seeing the "big picture." If you can't place the details of the material to be retained into a larger context, then the information will be scattered throughout your brain like fallen leaves blown about in autumn. Get the big picture first; it will help your understanding and memory.

A lack of motivation. If you don't see the point of memorizing something, you'll have a hard time putting forth the effort to do it. If you need to convince yourself of its importance, do it promptly. Your time is valuable. Perhaps you dislike a particular class and find it boring, but it's required for your major. It's crucial that you motivate yourself to study for it. Think of the result of your efforts, and you'll realize that it's a good cause.

Turning these points around, here are the first four things you can do to improve your memory:

- Pay attention and focus on what is being presented.
- Realize that understanding comes before retention.
- Remember that it's more effective to fit details into the "big picture" than haphazardly.
- Convince yourself that it's important to memorize the material.

SIX TOOLS FOR BUILDING A BETTER MEMORY

Many educators say that memory aids have no place in education, claiming that as long as you understand something you'll remember it. *Wrong!* Memory aids are very valuable in helping you retain concepts and their supporting facts. They can save you time and increase your retention dramatically.

I recommend six memory tools, or mnemonics, that can improve your ability to store and retain material. They worked for me when I was in school, they've worked for many of my patients, they work for Chloe and Alizé, and they can work for you, too. All of these methods involve using associations between information already possessed and the information that needs to be stored. These techniques will help you become an active learner, and any time you combine activity with study, your chances of retention are greater.

Memory Tool #1: How to remember dates and numbers

The first of these mnemonics is a very helpful tool that's been around for over a century. Professor A. Loisette wrote about it in his book *Assimilative Memory or How to Attend and Never Forget*, which was published back in 1896. This technique provides a simple code for translating numbers into certain letters. This makes it easy to remember any series of numbers by just making up words or sentences using the letters that correspond with the numbers. Here's one example of this system:

Number	Consonant(s)	Rationale
1	t, d	t has one downstroke, d looks like a 0 + 1 = 1
2	N	n has two downstrokes
3	M	m has three downstrokes
4	R	r is the fourth letter of "four"
5	L	capital L is the Roman numeral for 50
6	g, J	g looks like an upside-down down 6, and capital J looks like a backward 6
7	soft c	soft c starts with the same sound as 7
8	F	both 8 and cursive f have 2 loops
9	p, b	backward p or upside-down b looks like 9
0	z, s	z is the first letter of "zero"; s looks like a backward z

In this system, all other consonants and vowels have no number value. You can master this code in 10 minutes or less, and it will be one of the most profitable 600 seconds of your life! Once you've got it, you can then translate any number into a word or sequence of words that can be easily associated in your brain. Here are a couple examples:

TECH TIP FROM CHLOE AND ALIZÉ
If you have trouble remembering important dates, you can easily enter holidays, birthdays, and appointments in your smartphone calendar and set reminders to alert you when those days arrive.

- If you need to remember that gold melts at 1,943 degrees Fahrenheit, recall "This bullion really melts." The first letter of each word is t = 1, b = 9, r = 4, m = 3. (Note: A gold bar is also called a gold bullion.)
- If you need to remember that the coldest temperature ever recorded in Antarctica is –89 degrees Celsius, recall the first letters of "freezing butt": f = 8, b = 9.

You can use your keys as the first letter of each word in a phrase, or as all of the keyed letters in a single word. Use this technique to remember dates, times, or other numbers.

Memory Tool #2: Rhyme to remember

Rhymes are a very popular tool for recalling rules or organization. For example, think of these common rhymes you may have learned as a child:

- I before E except after C.
- Spring ahead, fall back.
- In 1492, Columbus sailed the ocean blue.

Rhymes help connect items that may otherwise seem completely unrelated into a metrical pattern. They are very good at establishing definite orders, because any mistake in the order of recall will destroy the rhyme.

There's another way you can use rhyme to aid in retaining a sequence of facts. First memorize these simple rhymes:

- 1 is a bun
- 2 is a shoe
- 3 is a tree
- 4 is a door
- 5 is a hive
- 6 are sticks
- 7 is heaven
- 8 is a gate
- 9 is a line
- 10 is a hen

Now you can choose up to 10 facts you need to remember in a precise order and mentally picture an association between each of them and their corresponding number's object. In less than a few minutes you can easily memorize their order. Try this method with unrelated facts to observe its usefulness to you. For example, let's say you have to remember the six wives of England's King Henry VIII in order from first to last. Here's how you could do it:

1. Catherine of Aragon: She ate a bun and now it's gone. (last part of Aragon)
2. Anne Boleyn: She wore bowlin' shoes. (sounds like Boleyn)
3. Jane Seymour: She climbed a tree so she could see more. (see more = Seymour)
4. Anne of Cleves: She leaves through the door. (leaves sounds like "Cleves")
5. Catherine Howard: Her last name starts with the same letter as hive.

6. Catherine Paar: She shot par with her golf sticks (aka clubs). (par sounds like "Paar")

Memory Tool #3: Use places to remember specific things

The Greek poet Simonides was said to have left a banquet just before the roof collapsed, killing all those inside. Many of the bodies were unrecognizable, but Simonides was able to identify them by remembering their place at the table.

The practical use of the "loci method" involves placing an associative object in a certain location. Then by going back in your mind to the location, the object or fact should come back to you. For example, in memorizing a speech that is organized and outlined, choose the ideas or the major subdivisions and associate them in some way with the different rooms in your home. As you're delivering the speech, imagine yourself walking from room to room discovering the associations you have made in the proper order. Here's an example for a speech on the five major regions of the brain:

Brain Region	Room	Association
Prefrontal cortex	Front door	Start at the front door for the pre*front*al cortex.
Temporal lobe	Living room	The temporal lobe is involved in auditory processing, and you listen to music in your living room.
Parietal lobe	Kitchen	The parietal lobe is involved in sensory processing, like the tastes and smells of cooking in the kitchen.
Occipital lobe	Family room	The occipital lobe is involved in visual processing, like when you watch TV in the family room.
Cerebellum	Backyard	The cerebellum is involved in motor coordination, like when you play catch in the backyard.

If you practice this technique, your associative powers will become limited only by the number of locations you can imagine.

Memory Tool #4: Use acronyms or initialisms

Using acronyms (words like NASA that are formed from the initial letters of words) can be very helpful. Similarly, initialisms use the first letters of words, but they do not form a pronounceable word (like that wacky sentence at the beginning of this chapter). When I have a series of facts to memorize, the first thing I do is examine their first letters to see if I can arrange them into an associative word or phrase. In general, the more colorful, the greater the chance it will be easily remembered. Here is an example of this method:

"On old Olympus's towering top, a Finn and German viewed a hop." Each first letter corresponds to the first letter of the 12 cranial nerves in their proper order: olfactory, optic, oculomotor, trochlear, trigeminal, abducens, facial, acoustic, glossopharyngeal, vagus, accessory, and hypoglossal.

Time for a pop quiz! Can you remember the example of an initialism I used at the beginning of this chapter? If not, feel free to go back to that page to review its superb qualities.

In my academic and professional career, I have compiled well over 1,000 of these sentences. Even though I don't recall all of them, I remembered them when exam day arrived or for as long as I needed them. Practice this method. Your memory will thank you!

Memory Tool #5: Create pictures to boost your memory

Did you know that about 30 percent of the brain's neurons are devoted to visual processing, while only 8 percent are dedicated to touch and a paltry 3 percent to hearing? Because the mind thinks in images, it can be very helpful to create pictures to remember information. Constructing big pictures with central figures and supporting details also fits the theme of this book. It is important to keep three things in mind when forming these images:

- Include action, since your brain thinks in movies rather than in still photographs. The more action there is, the more details you can employ in a scene.
- Make the picture as weird and offbeat as possible. It will be easier to remember the details as you recall the strange or unique things in the picture.
- Associate the overall theme of the scene with something that will allow you to remember why it is related to the concepts or details found in it. See the below example.

One of the best mnemonic images I ever created was for the infective organism chlamydia, which is responsible for causing at least five ailments: elephantiasis (severe swelling of the leg), lymphogranuloma venereum (a venereal disease), pneumonia, anal abnormalities, and a disease termed "parrot fever." In the image I created, the scene's locale is the bottom of the ocean where a large clam (chlamydia) is sitting. On top of the clam stands an elephant (elephantiasis) with Elvie (pronounced LV for lymphogranuloma venereum), an acquaintance of mine, sitting on her back, coughing (pneumonia). Now Elvie had a reputation for excessive hip movement, and that is how the association with anal abnormalities is made. Finally, perched on her shoulder is a talkative parrot (parrot fever) who is ready to tell Elvie about any new discoveries that medicine makes with chlamydia, leaving room to expand the information in the picture when it becomes necessary. I have retained the details of this image for several years and have found this technique a significant aid to my memory.

Memory Tool #6: Make connections

The last mnemonic method involves finding sets of connections for information that needs to be stored. This can be in the form of combining any of the previous five techniques or by employing number and letter sets. All that is involved in these sets is the recall of the number of items in a group: "There are nine circles of hell in Dante's *Inferno*, and I have only six; I must think of three more." This technique works even better with long lists broken into lettered groups. For example, let's say your science teacher wants you to memorize the 10 basic types of clouds:

Low-Level Clouds

- Cumulus
- Cumulonimbus
- Stratocumulus
- Stratus

Mid-Level Clouds

- Altocumulus
- Altostratus
- Nimbostratus

High-Level Clouds

- Cirrus
- Cirrocumulus
- Cirrostratus

It can seem like a random list to recall, but if you remember that five of them start with C, two of them start with A, two of them start with S, and one of them starts with N, it will be easier to recall all of them. This is a simple tool, and if you can find these similarities, your work will be easier. If you have too many sets to remember, this method can be confusing, but combining this method with others will help alleviate that problem.

It is helpful to begin forming these mnemonics at the first exposure to the material, as this allows time to find associations. It might not always be easy to find associations initially, but usually you can find one or more of the six categories into which you can place the material. Be versatile and use any method that works for you.

The power of mnemonics is in their ability to reduce long, unrelated strings of information into short, related lists. Practice the techniques! If you invest time in training your memory, the work will save you from boring repetition. If you're not having a particularly creative time, however, then repeat the information until you know it. At least with repetition you are being active with the material, and activity is a prerequisite to learning.

This chapter can be summarized with four rules for efficient memorization:

- Pay attention to what you're learning.
- Process the material internally, ensuring that it fits together in a logical sequence and that you understand its whole.
- Establish a relationship between the material you want to learn and material you already possess—association is key.
- Realize that any mental activity performed on material, such as forming pictures, rhymes, or acronyms, increases the depth of processing and automatically helps you form connections that improve retrievability.

CHANGE YOUR BRAIN, CHANGE YOUR GRADES: PARIETAL RELATIONS

- Association is the key to memory.
- Immediate memory initially intakes material and is enhanced by focusing attention on the material to be remembered.
- Short-term memory is the temporary storage place for information and is enhanced by concentration, grouping, and understanding.
- Long-term memory is just that—long-term storage of material—and is initially dependent on immediate and short-term memory.
- Memory usually fails because of an initial lack of focus, understanding, context, or motivation.
- Mnemonics will improve your recall. Learn how to use them to your advantage.
- Repetition is useful if your associative powers dim.

10

TWO HEADS ARE BETTER THAN NONE

Studying with a Partner

Y̲ou've heard the proverb "Two heads are better than one." Well, I say that two heads are better than *none*. Often there is "no head" at work trying to learn, assimilate, or memorize information because you're lost, bogged down, or bored by what you're doing. With two heads working together, you can eliminate most of these problems and make far greater progress. In this chapter, you'll learn the reasons for studying with another person, the best ways to choose a study buddy, and the most effective methods for group study—including why you should keep your group to only two or three people at most.

Why Study with Someone Else?

Studying with a partner can be valuable for many reasons, such as increasing your understanding of the material, getting better grades, and establishing strong and lasting friendships (not necessarily in that order). Studying with another person also helps break the monotony of rigorous, solitary study. Simply put, it's usually more fun to have someone "suffer" with you, and anything that is fun usually results in increased time spent on that activity.

GETTING SOCIAL: ONE OF THE 4 CIRCLES OF A HEALTHY BRAIN AND LIFE

When I was in medical school, the dean, Dr. Sid Garrett, gave a lecture on how to help people of any age for any problem. What he said has stuck with me ever since. Dr. Garrett told us, "Always think of people as whole beings, never just as their symptoms." In his view, when treating someone, we should always take into consideration the four circles of health and illness:

- **Biological:** how your physical body functions (body and BRIGHT MINDS factors)
- **Psychological:** developmental issues and how you think (mind)
- **Social:** social support and your current life situation (connections)
- **Spiritual:** your sense of meaning and purpose (spirit)

At Amen Clinics, we use these four circles to take a balanced, comprehensive approach to optimizing brain health. Having a good study partner plays into the social circle and can help you deal with school stresses as well as other life challenges. Having this type of social support can bolster your brain in many ways.

Studying together helps clarify weak areas. By sharing your notes, each of you will be able to pick up points you missed, fill in the gaps in your notes, and come to a better understanding of what material was emphasized in class. It's easier to look up questions when two people benefit from the information and can share the information-finding chore. If you can't make sense of the material together, you'll need the help of your instructor.

Having a lively, humorous, or just plain compatible partner makes it so much easier to press on when you want to shove off. Keeping each other motivated is a major benefit. Besides, having someone to talk to and bounce ideas off of will keep you awake through those long study sessions.

The last reason for studying with a partner is that you can see how your partner studies, which gives you an opportunity to incorporate new and different methods into your study arsenal. Ultimately, it can improve your overall study skills.

In my experience with study partners, I benefited the most when:

TECH TIP FROM CHLOE AND ALIZÉ

One of the best things about group study is you can divvy up the research. This means you only have to spend half as much time scouring the internet while still getting 100 percent of the information you need.

- They told me what they perceived to be the main thoughts on the subject matter.
- They told me what they thought the test questions would be.
- I compared their thoughts to my own. I was likely to miss several important points (as was my partner), but by comparing our knowledge and insights, we were both able to have a more complete overall picture.
- I heard information repeated and answered questions aloud before the exam. Seeing and hearing information improves retention tremendously!

CHOOSING YOUR STUDY PARTNER

Now that you know that studying with another person is beneficial, how do you go about finding a good partner? Choose carefully, because the right partner can help you reap tremendous benefits, while the wrong partner can really screw up your progress and your grades! Here's what to look for in a good study buddy.

Look for equality and compatibility. Finding a study partner is sort of like choosing a mate. You're going to be spending a lot of time together, so it's important that your time is enjoyable and productive. Make sure the person you're considering shares some of the same study habits or similar ones. If you prefer to study at 6 o'clock in the morning so you can head to the gym before class and they prefer to study at midnight on the way home from a party, it's probably not going to work. You need to find someone of equal intelligence, speed of comprehension, and style of organization. Otherwise, the person with good study skills ends up acting as a tutor, which is not the intent of this method. (You'll learn more about the value of tutoring later.)

Try a few partners. Spend the first part of the semester studying with a few different people until you find someone who is in your league in terms of intellect, skillset, and motivation. Don't dive headfirst into a study relationship; it takes time to find the right person, so check out your options.

> ### TECH TIP FROM CHLOE AND ALIZÉ
>
> Think of choosing a study partner like those dating apps that let you swipe right or swipe left to accept or reject a person. Go on lots of "study dates" at the beginning of the semester until you find a study partner who's a good match for you.

Find someone with the same major or interest in the same field. Make sure that you find someone with whom you enjoy working, especially someone in your major field of study. Then you'll have more than one course to study together.

Reliability counts. It is very important to make sure that your partner is reliable and diligent in your work together. If they are chronically ill prepared for your sessions, or have not appeared for the third consecutive study session, it's time to find another partner.

Two is the magic number. Keep your study group to two people and definitely no more than three at the most. Larger groups are for parties and prayer meetings, but not for studying. You'll quickly discover that even with three people together, you'll have trouble pacing yourself and staying on track.

Don't choose someone simply because you'd like to date them. Yes, I said to think of the search for a study partner like looking for a mate, but dating isn't the real goal. If you find yourself attracted to your study partner, your brain will release chemicals and hormones that will distract you from your studies and make it harder for you to learn the material. Choose someone you like, but not someone you'll fall in love with.

**TECH TIP FROM
CHLOE AND ALIZÉ**
If you've chosen a good study partner and you enjoy working together but your schedules don't match up all the time, use FaceTime, Skype, Google Hangouts, or any other online video conferencing apps and sites. A study session on the computer is better than none!

METHODS FOR STUDYING WITH A PARTNER

To get the most out of studying with a partner, follow these guidelines.

Be prepared. Each partner should have a set of rewritten notes and should read them once before getting together. When reading your notes and assigned reading material beforehand, observe any areas that you're missing, any concepts you don't understand, and any ideas you think are especially important. Come to the study session prepared to give, instruct, and clarify these points with your partner. You will leave reinforced and informed.

Teach each other. If you can teach something, you know it. If each of you comes to the study session as if you were going to teach it, you will both come away with a solid understanding.

Set time limits for your sessions. You probably have other subjects to tackle, so set a start and an end time for your sessions. Take adequate breaks during your sessions to keep yourself fresh, but remember your purpose and minimize the lengthy chats. In general, it's a good rule to take a 10-minute break after 50 minutes of study. The achievement of good grades and learning requires 50 minutes per hour.

Take turns. Once you and your partner have discussed what you want to accomplish in your session and have a good set of notes and questions in front of you, simply take turns reading aloud, reviewing, or questioning each other on the material in a systematic way. Be sure to leave time for discussion of the misunderstood points. If areas of question arise, try to answer them quickly. If the answer is not readily available, jot it down to ask the professor and move on. Get through the material once quickly and decide what needs more work. When going through the subject matter, alternate with your partner and be sure you've gone through all the material at least twice. In the first round, you expound on the material and ask the questions. In the second round, you listen and answer questions.

Create your own test questions. Devise questions as you go along, trying to anticipate what questions will be on the exam. This is a good study method when studying alone and is enhanced with two heads. You can also write down your unanswered questions as you go along and have a "scavenger hunt" later to see who can find the answer first. Also, when studying together, try to create parietal pictures. As you recall from chapter 9, parietal pictures are kooky, exaggerated mental pictures to aid your memory. Your joint effort will enhance their quality.

Minimize distractions. All of the other rules and ideas for good study techniques, such as minimizing distractions, apply when studying together. So don't study in front of the television or in a room with loud music.

Recap and review. After you've covered the material, clarified points, and noted questions for the professor, be sure to restate the main points and review them. Have one person make a list (make sure you have two copies) with the major points and facts that you can use for a quick review.

It's okay to get personal. At the beginning of this chapter, I mentioned that one of the advantages of studying with a partner was the establishment of strong and lasting friendships. I remember the many hours I spent studying with some really amazing people. The fellowship and empathy we shared made those times some of my most precious memories. Keep in mind that we are relational beings, and if we can enhance our study skills and establish positive, reinforcing relationships at the same time, we indeed have a powerful tool.

Move on if it isn't working. If the sound of the other person's voice drives you up the wall, you hate the way they fidget in their chair, or you get annoyed by everything they do, then your study skills will diminish. If your sessions aren't as productive as you'd like them to be and you don't see a way to work together to improve them, it's time to call it quits and find a new study partner.

CHANGE YOUR BRAIN, CHANGE YOUR GRADES: TWO HEADS ARE BETTER THAN NONE

- Reasons for studying with another person include increasing your understanding, clarifying information, comparing notes and impressions on the important points, and seeing how your partner studies.
- Equality and compatibility are the two main criteria in choosing a partner.
- Ideally, study with only one other person at a time, and never more than two.
- When studying together, be prepared for your session, set time limits and stick to them, create test questions, make a recap list, and examine material quickly at first and in detail later.
- The establishment of strong and lasting relationships is an important and beneficial byproduct of studying with a partner.

11

GO TO THE SOURCE

A Practical Approach to Teachers

During my 21 years as a student, I had many outstanding instructors. For example, my pathology professor epitomized the essence of inspired teaching. He taught in an organized, concise, interesting, and humorous fashion that made his class presentations pertinent and practical.

This special professor made learning a tough subject enjoyable. He also encouraged close relationships between his students and himself. I remember piling into his car with three other classmates to go to a funeral home in Henryetta, Oklahoma, to perform our first autopsy. He was the master pathologist, and by cultivating a close relationship with him, we learned more than the "dead facts." We began to understand the workings of a superb pathologist's mind in solving medical problems. This concept has tremendous value. You can get the facts from any good textbook, but you can only see how it is done firsthand by observation. Cultivating solid relationships with your instructors is basic to learning more than the bare facts.

As you've seen in this book, your teachers can be a tremendous resource to you. This topic is so important that I have devoted a full chapter to it so you can learn how to take full advantage of the student-teacher relationship. This chapter is divided into three sections:

- **Part 1** deals with the value you can derive from your instructor before the class actually begins.
- **Part 2** discusses the aspects of a productive student-teacher relationship during the course.
- **Part 3** deals with the interaction you might want to have with the instructor after the class is completed.

PART 1: ENGAGE YOUR TEACHER BEFORE THE COURSE BEGINS

Approaching the professor before a class begins can be valuable for a number of reasons, including the following.

1. It helps you establish rapport with the professor, thereby making you more than just a face without a name in class. This is the first step in establishing a relationship with the professor. This practice has value even if there are more than 100 students in a class because after you have approached an instructor once, you will feel more comfortable approaching them again. If you're hesitant or fearful to approach your teacher, remember that they are there to help you become the best doctor, lawyer, communications specialist, entrepreneur, bioengineer, computer scientist, child psychologist, creative writer, or whatever it is you want to be in life. Getting acquainted with your teachers is the first step toward building a valuable relationship with them.

2. You may have a lot of questions about a course, such as: *What is this class all about? Do I have the adequate prerequisites? How much study time does the professor think will be needed for this course? What sources other than the textbook are helpful?* It can be helpful to have these questions answered before the class begins so you can be better prepared for the class.

3. The beginning of the course is also a good time to ask the teacher for suggestions on how to approach the subject. As experts in the subject, they should be able to direct you to the best ways for you to assimilate the material they're presenting. After all, one of the definitions of the word *teach* in Merriam-Webster's Collegiate Dictionary is "to guide the

KNOW YOUR TEACHER'S BRAIN TYPE

In addition to knowing your own brain type, it is a good idea to know the brain type of the important people in your life, and that includes your teachers. Understanding their brain type gives you better insight into how to approach them for help. Based on our brain imaging work at Amen Clinics, we have identified 5 primary brain types:

- *Brain Type 1: Balanced*—Teachers who have a balanced brain tend to be flexible and easy to approach.
- *Brain Type 2: Spontaneous*—Teachers with a spontaneous brain are more likely to be fun-loving and to appreciate creativity. Stretch yourself in these classes and try thinking "outside the box" on your assignments to appeal to this type.
- *Brain Type 3: Persistent*—Teachers who have this brain type are typically "my way or the highway" kind of people. Don't attempt to argue with them and be sure to stick within their guidelines to do best in their classes.
- *Brain Type 4: Sensitive*—Teachers who have a sensitive brain tend to look at the negative side of things. Cheering them up with a positive spin on a subject can help.
- *Brain Type 5: Cautious*—Teachers with this brain type are more likely to be anxious. For better results and interactions with this type, don't fuel their anxiety.

studies of." So let teachers do their job by letting them show you how to study their subject.

4. For college students, approaching the instructor before a class begins gives you the advantage of dropping the class early if you find that you aren't adequately prepared for it, if it isn't what you expected, or for any other reason. This may sound like a negative suggestion, but dropping a class early is much smarter than dropping it three weeks into the semester. At that late date, it can be very hard to replace it with another class, and even if you do, you'll be three weeks behind in that class when

you start it. As soon as possible, you should establish if the class you're taking is what you expected and what you can handle.

PART 2: MASTERING THE STUDENT-TEACHER RELATIONSHIPS DURING THE COURSE

Developing a productive student-teacher relationship during a course involves five major areas: approaching, questioning, notes, tests, and ways of enhancing the relationship.

1. Learn how to approach your instructors. Remember that you have a right to expect certain things from your instructors. It is reasonable to expect organized and interesting lectures that have some practical value. It is fair to assume that the instructor's job involves helping you master the techniques of learning the subject. It is reasonable to expect to be treated fairly and with dignity during lectures and laboratory sessions as well as in grading.

When approaching the instructor, be humble and open to suggestions. Acting arrogant or giving the impression that you already know everything is counterproductive. Most teachers enter the field because they feel that they have something of value to give to students. If you approach them thinking they are there to support your preconceived ideas or just to give you a good grade, then you will invariably have trouble with them. However, if your attitude is one of respect for the teacher as well as enthusiasm for the subject at hand, you can gain from a productive relationship.

If you're having misunderstandings or problems with a professor, approach them with a group of students to discuss the grievances. On the first day of medical school I was randomly chosen by my anatomy professor to chair a student grievance committee. He felt students needed a collective voice to deal with any class problems. As it evolved, the committee served three main purposes.

- It was valuable in giving positive and negative (but constructive) feedback to the teachers regarding their lectures, including whether or not class material was being understood by the students.

- The committee functioned after exams to question the validity of certain questions and their answers. This was very productive, because the committee was able to have answers revised or questions deleted, thus raising the curve of the test by more than 10 points on several occasions.
- We sat with different course directors and discussed the overall effectiveness of the class. This committee was very productive and operated symbiotically between teachers and students.

If you have questions, put forth some effort to understand the concept before using your instructor as a sounding board. In my committee, if we had questions, we tried to research the answer first. If we still did not understand, then we went ahead and asked. Conversely, if you expect the teacher to take you through the concept step by step without doing any research, you are likely to be viewed unfavorably.

2. Asking questions and dialoguing are integral parts of the learning process, and these skills need to be cultivated continually. Your approach to the professor, as mentioned above, is of the utmost importance in this regard. Also, doing your part in researching material that is not well understood is crucial to having any meaningful dialogue on the questions you might have throughout the course.

During a course, the first question to ask is, "Why am I taking this course, and how will it enhance my educational goals?" Since the professor has probably had many years of training on the subject, they should be able to give you the answer. Also, if you did not talk to the professor before the class began, this is a good time to ask questions about how to approach the subject matter. In addition, if you need a certain grade in a class, this is the appropriate time to ask the instructor how to get it. The more information you have, the better chance you will have to obtain your goal.

The more you approach a teacher with well thought out and researched questions, the more they will be able to help you assimilate the material in a course. Use the time before and after class, as well as the teacher's office hours. Students who say they can never talk to the professor usually are not trying hard enough. Remember, teachers are the best source of help to you in learning the subject matter, so go to them with your questions.

If you have the backup of a student grievance committee, that's great; if not, you should still approach the professor with questions or feedback that you might have. By all means, if you have a question on a test you have taken, challenge (after researching) the answer that the professor keyed as the right one.

> **TECH TIP FROM CHLOE AND ALIZÉ**
> Be sure to get your professor's email address so you can send them questions or concerns. Don't overuse it though! Wait until you have all your questions and send a single email rather than filling their inbox with question after question.

3. As suggested earlier, try to get a copy of the teacher's lecture notes before the lecture. This will give you valuable information on what is important and help keep writer's cramps at bay during the lecture. Also, it will give you the assurance of having complete notes and will be helpful in guiding you to organize your notes. Do not neglect this valuable source of information. Even if the teacher will not let you copy their notes, you still will gain from the interaction by demonstrating to the instructor your interest and desire to do well in the class.

4. As far as tests are concerned, it is wise to have as much information on them as possible before the exam. Most teachers will gladly tell you what they expect from you on a test and will give you many helpful clues on how to prepare for the exam. So try to obtain as much information on the content of the exams as the instructor will give you.

5. Remember that teachers are people too. Another worthwhile goal to have during the semester is that of enhancing your relationships with your faculty. We are all relational beings and need to interact on a human level. Spend time getting to know your professors, their backgrounds, and their professional and personal goals. We learn from their lives as well as from the lecture material. This is especially true if the teacher is in a discipline you might enter. You can learn so much more from your professors, and your relationships with them will be cherished long after you have forgotten 80 percent of the details they gave you in class!

Also, this relationship will be valuable to you in the future if you need letters of recommendation from your teachers. This certainly is not the most important reason for establishing lasting relationships with your instructors, but you will probably need these letters in the future, and it is very beneficial to get them from a teacher who knows you.

PART 3: YOUR EFFORT SHOULDN'T END WHEN THE CLASS ENDS

When the class is nearing its end or has finished, you have three major responsibilities.

1. You have the responsibility of evaluating the class honestly for future students. This gives the teacher valuable feedback on their performance. It has been my experience that teachers are genuinely interested in students' suggestions for improvement. Students are generally too kind in their evaluations, not wanting to hurt the instructor's feelings or not wanting to jeopardize their grade or recommendation. It does no good, and it is even harmful, to rate a class better than it was. If your honesty will affect your grade or recommendation, then turn it in anonymously, or wait until after the grades are posted to return it. This is your way of grading the professor; see how it feels!

2. You have the responsibility of obtaining letters of recommendation for yourself for future use. These are best

---

🖥️

TECH TIP FROM CHLOE AND ALIZÉ

If you want to rate your professor or get a preview of what a professor or class is like, visit www.ratemyprofessors.com. Submissions are anonymous.

written right after you have taken a course. The professor knows you and your work and will be able to write a more personal letter for you. The first step in obtaining this letter is to ask the professors of your choice (the more the better) if they would write you a positive letter of recommendation. If someone hedges, let them off the hook—you don't want noncommittal letters. If they agree, then ask for a copy of the letter so you can read it and decide whether or not you'll be able to use it. If you use this method, your letters of recommendation will have more meaning, and thus be superior to letters written two years after your last contact with the professor. Also, if you're asking for a letter of recommendation for a college or grad school application, be sure to ask for it well in advance of the application deadline. Giving a teacher ample time to craft the letter will usually result in a stronger recommendation.

3. It is your responsibility to obtain the best possible grade in the class. Some people say that you shouldn't be concerned with grades, or that they aren't a true measure of your knowledge. College and graduate school admissions boards, however, are keenly aware of your grades, and they use them to compare you with thousands of other applicants. If you can get a better grade, it is certainly worth a try. An extra effort is especially helpful if you are on the borderline between an A and a B or a B and a C.

Here are two strategies I have successfully used to obtain a higher grade in borderline situations:

- Ask for a higher grade due to the competitiveness of your major or career goals. If it is possible and fair, most teachers want to see their students become successful. So if they can in good conscience give you the higher grade, they will.
- Try gently pointing out the injustice of giving someone with an 89.9 percent average a B while at the same time giving an A to someone with a 90.1 percent average. In my case, it worked, but obviously, this does not always work, as illustrated in a *Peanuts* cartoon I once read. In it, Peppermint Patty wonders out loud to her teacher how the letter D by itself is a wonderful, important, and dignified letter. "When a minus is put behind

it," she argues, "it loses its dignity, appears drained, and has lost its power and strength." Her teacher would not change her grade but promised if she was ever on trial for her life, she would want Peppermint Patty for her lawyer.

If you never try to raise your grade or seem concerned about it, then the professor will assume that grades are not important to you, and they will not feel bad about giving you the lower grade. If, however, you make your desires known to your teachers, they will at least give your request some thought. Starting from the very first day of class, it is your job to establish with your teacher the kind of student you are and your goals. And most importantly, you need to follow through! This practice can make a significant difference in your grade point average. If you never try to talk a police officer out of a speeding ticket, then you will always simply take what they give you. But if you try to talk your way out of a ticket, you might have a 20 percent chance of succeeding. Over a lifetime, that is significant; the same is true of your GPA.

I opened this chapter by writing about a superb pathology professor; I will close by telling you about another professor I had. This instructor was similar to the first one in that his lectures were organized, practical, and interesting. He also encouraged close relationships with his students and served as a role model and mentor to many of us. He was secure enough to share with us some of his shortcomings and how he learned from the mistakes he had made in his career. He hoped to help us avoid some of the pain that accompanies mistakes. He also taught us that there is more to us than our studies—that to be happy and fulfilled, we need to cultivate other areas of our lives that have value, such as our family and social relationships, our physical well-being, and our intellectual and cultural growth. He taught us from his knowledge and from his life, and the gift of himself that he gave to us was more valuable than any other source of information available!

CHANGE YOUR BRAIN, CHANGE YOUR GRADES: GO TO THE SOURCE

- There are many advantages to cultivating relationships with your professors.
- Approach your instructors before a course begins to establish a rapport with them, have questions answered, learn how to approach the class, and drop the class early if it is not suitable for you.
- A student's attitude toward teachers should include expecting quality lectures, getting help from them, and being treated with dignity. Students should approach teachers with a humble and teachable spirit, come to them with a group when trouble arises, and ask questions after doing some preliminary research.
- During a course, the professor will be able to answer your questions, guide your studies and note-taking, and provide necessary information for upcoming exams.
- As a class is coming to an end, your responsibilities include evaluating it honestly, obtaining letters of recommendation, and discussing your grade if you think it should be higher.

12

PRESSURIZE YOUR CABIN

PREPARING FOR AND TAKING TESTS

Pressure has long been known to have strange effects on people, especially students. The pressure of exams is one of the most severe tests of a student's ability to cope under stress. Students have been known to buckle during strenuous times, doing things like staying awake three nights before an exam to cram 60 pages of math theorems and formulas that they have never seen before, eating coffee grounds to keep their eyelids open long enough to memorize the number of ribs on a female catfish, or popping "smart pills" to try to enhance their cognitive powers.

There is no doubt that for most students, test time is an anxious period filled with certain unavoidable pressures. The trick is to have the extra adrenaline and pressure work in your favor instead of driving you to act foolish. You can either let the excess energy help motivate you to prepare adequately for your upcoming task or let it feed your delusions that somehow God will send an angel to dictate the test answers to you.

This chapter is about regulating pressure under the load of exams. It has been said on more than one occasion that I received a high mark on an exam because of my skill at taking exams, not because of my knowledge. I think some of those comments might have been derogatory, but I took them as a compliment. If a B student operates at an A level on exams, that student will see more open doors and have more choices for future goals.

Unfortunately, the opposite fact is more often true. Students who know the material well often achieve a lower grade on an exam because of poor test-taking skills, not because their knowledge is lacking. Knowing the material well is only part of being a good test-taker. There are established skills in test preparation, test-taking, alleviation of test anxiety, and review of exams once they are graded.

Much of this book has been geared to prepare you for exams, so you will find some repetition in this chapter. However, as someone once said, "Repetition is the mother of education." I guess I did not repeat that person's name enough . . . (Just kidding! It was John Paul Richter in 1807.)

A TIMELINE FOR PREPARING FOR EXAMS

It's very important to understand that there is usually no correlation between the amount of time studied and the grade on a test. Your study methods and test-taking techniques will decide the outcome of the exam. This section on preparing for exams is divided into four parts:

- Several weeks before the exam
- Several days before the exam
- The day before the exam
- The day of the exam

Several Weeks Before the Exam

1. Set up a study schedule and stick to it. The first thing to do when starting a new class is to set up a study schedule that will allow you enough time to learn the material adequately. The time to begin preparing for the first exam is at the beginning of the class. I tried to arrange my study schedule so I would be ready to take the exam three days *before* it was actually given. This gave me the opportunity right before the exam to study with a partner and obtain their insights, ask the professor any last-minute questions I still had, and leave my overall study schedule intact. This way, I wasn't

neglecting everything else in my life. Even though I didn't always achieve this goal, I aimed for it. This approach keeps you from feeling that you have to pull an all-nighter right before the test.

TECH TIP FROM CHLOE AND ALIZÉ

Input your study schedule in your phone's calendar and set reminders and alerts to help you stick to it.

2. Study in units that are organized and concise. This will give you an advantage in your review because you'll know how much material you have covered and how much is left to tackle. Also engage in periodic overall reviews. Take time once a week to briefly review all of the material that you have studied for a new section, and you'll find that the review before the exam will go much faster, because the material will be fresh in your memory, and you will have assimilated more of it.

3. Make sure you have a complete set of lecture notes. For most classes, about 75 percent of the test questions come directly from the lecture material. Recopy your notes soon after class to complete them, improve their neatness, and give you more exposure to them. Your notes are usually your best guide to studying for an exam.

4. Keep a separate sheet of the test questions that you have created on the studied material. As you saw in chapter 8, devising your own questions boosts active learning and helps you recognize important concepts and facts. If you keep a record of these facts, they will be helpful during your review.

5. Create a "big picture" fact sheet. On your fact sheet, list only the major concepts and their supporting facts, along with any formulas or key words that you would find useful in a very quick review. I used to write this sheet as I did my initial studies, and it would never total more than three to four pages in length. It was very useful for a one- to two-hour review, and it was ideal for study prior to the exam.

6. At least one week before the exam, ask your professor the "Four Whats":

- What specific topics are going to be covered on the exam?

- What material will be emphasized on the test?
- What type of questions will be on the test? (This often will give you important clues on how to prepare for the exam.)
- What clues can the professor give you for preparing for the test?

Many teachers are willing to guide students in their review for exams. It is not only impractical to try to study everything that you have been taught in the whole semester before an exam, but you will likely remember absolutely nothing on test day. It is much more sensible to find out as much as possible about the exam from the teacher; after all, they are the exam's source.

Several Days Before the Exam

This is often the pressure cooker time for many students, but if you follow these simple principles, you'll be able to harness the steam to help your brain work more efficiently.

1. Study effectively with a partner. As you have seen, this will help you have motivation and stamina for review while giving you another perspective on the exam material. This time can also be used for clarifying questionable material, and you'll have the opportunity to use someone else as a sounding board to measure your understanding of it.

2. Attend the classes right before the exam. Many students think that this is the time to skip class to get in a few extra hours of study. During the last few class sessions before an exam, however, the teacher usually gives important information about the upcoming test. This time is also very useful in class, because if new material is presented, its proximity to the exam will help you retain it. Remember, your best source for exams is your lecture notes, so go to class to the end and take notes.

3. Have a good attitude and confident mindset when you study. This reduces stress and allows your brain to function at more optimal levels.

4. Continue to revise and update your "big picture" fact sheet. During your review, if you get bogged down in the details, go to the "big picture" of what you're studying. If you have a solid foundation for the main ideas,

you can build with the facts. If you're trying to nail facts onto a flimsy base, you'll certainly discover your knowledge broken or splintered.

5. Harness the cram monster and make it work for you! Many educators will tell you that cramming before an exam reveals poor study habits. I disagree. Cramming is worthwhile and, if used correctly, can dramatically increase your test score. The trick is to use cramming for review, not first exposure. If you're cramming material that you have never seen before, you will find yourself in big trouble. Intensive study of material that has been partially assimilated, however, will increase your short-term memory of it and thus help you on exams. Many studies have shown that the major factor in retention for exams is recentness of exposure to the material. So cram what you know; you'll learn it better and remember it longer. Scan over your materials and if you happen to see a subject that requires additional review, study it more thoroughly, maybe make some sticky notes, and keep going!

6. If, for whatever reason, you find yourself in the position of cramming cold material just before an exam, here are a few hints to help you weather the inevitable storm:

- Make sure that you know the lecture notes.
- Read the chapter introductions, topic sentences, graphs, italicized words, and most importantly the chapter summaries.
- If your professor allows this, try to get a copy of old exams to see what material was emphasized previously (which is a good idea even if you know the material).
- Get a review book that gives you just the bare facts of the section and review from that.

The Day Before the Exam

Use this time for an overall quick review of the material, relying on your notes and "big picture" fact sheets." Review these at least twice—once to learn what areas still need polishing and a second time to be exposed to the material one last time.

Your study habits aren't the only thing that will make a difference on exam day. Your lifestyle habits can also impact your performance. Eat a healthy diet (more on this in chapter 15) in the days and weeks before your test and be sure to get a full night's sleep before an exam. Not only will you feel more refreshed and energized the following morning, but memories are also consolidated in the brain while you snooze.

The Day of the Exam

It is a good idea to have something to eat before the exam, but don't pig out because your energy will wallow in the mud as the blood flow shifts from your brain to your stomach. A small portion of lean protein and a healthy fat, like avocado, is a good idea. Protein and fat take longer to burn off than carbs, which give you a quick boost of energy but will wear off fast. If the test is going to be an extended affair, bring a protein bar or some nuts into the exam room with you to increase your energy level, if necessary.

Arrive a few minutes before the exam begins and bring extra paper and writing materials. You don't want to be frazzled from the start and break your focus. If you arrive too early, then you will just have more time to kill, allowing your anxiety level to rise. If you're late, you'll have missed the instructions, putting you at a disadvantage from the start, which will make your anxiety level go through the roof!

Stay away from congregations of students right before the exam. Some "Nervous Nellie" will invariably bring up some picky detail you didn't study, thereby increasing your anxiety even though that factoid most likely won't appear on the test.

When you go into the exam room, try to find a seat that is as far away from distractions as possible. Usually this means not sitting in the front row, near doors or windows, or near a noisy test taker. I remember my first anatomy exam. I thought it would be a good idea to sit next to my best friend so that we could give each other emotional support. But, to my shock and distraction, he was the loudest test taker in the state of Oklahoma (a real "boomer Sooner")! His pencil blazed loudly across the test, and he breathed as though he was nourishing his brain with oxygen, as an engineer would feed his locomotive with coal. We stayed best of friends in medical school, but that was partially due to the fact that I had a choice of not sitting near him during exams.

One of the most important things to remember before starting an exam is to trust yourself. Trust that you know the answers and trust your judgment for the ones you don't remember. Once you're in your seat, there is no more last-minute studying—all you have is your brain to fall back on. Take a deep breath and trust yourself to get you through it.

THE 6 DON'TS OF TEST PREP

- *Don't skimp on sleep.* If you don't get enough sleep before a big test, you're more likely to forget what you studied the night before.
- *Don't rely on smart pills.* Taking so-called smart pills in hopes of a boost in energy, alertness, and memory can lead to long-term brain issues. Researchers say they can lead to difficulties multitasking, planning, and organizing.
- *Don't take your little brother's ADHD medication.* According to a 2018 study, ADHD drugs may fail to improve cognitive function in healthy students and may in fact impair functioning.[1]
- *Don't guzzle Red Bull, coffee, soda, or other caffeine-laden drinks.* Caffeine can give you an initial boost of energy and make you feel more alert, but when it wears off it can leave you feeling sluggish and give you brain fog.
- *Don't pig out on junk food.* Eating doughnuts, candy, or other junk foods before a test can give you brain fog.
- *Don't forget to hydrate.* Even mild dehydration can dull your concentration, reduce alertness, and give you a headache.

TAKING THE EXAM

Congratulations! You've made it to test day. Now it's time to get down to business and ace this thing. Here are some general test-taking tips that you'll find helpful, as well as recommendations for answering essay and objective questions.

General Test-Taking Tips

First, get an overview of the test to determine the number and types of questions. Then determine the approximate amount of time you have per question and divide your time appropriately.

Next, read the test instructions! I can't stress enough how important this is. They may tell you that you have to answer only a certain percentage of the questions on the test, or they may give you a choice of one of two essay questions.

Answer the questions you know first. This will ensure that you get credit for what you know if you run out of time. If you're unsure about any questions, mark them and return to them later. Remember that another question later in the test may give you valuable information for an earlier one.

Answer questions as you think the teacher would have you answer them.

Take questions at their face value. Sometimes you'll read a question and will know the answer right off the bat, but then you start to second-guess your instincts. And then you second-guess that, and the cycle continues until the teacher tells you to put pencils down. Trust your instinct.

Most teachers create tests that are straightforward and are not trying to fool you with hidden meanings or trick questions. If you have a question about some aspect of the test, ask the professor about it during the exam. If they don't want to answer the question, they'll tell you. Often, however, they will clear up confusing points for you.

Finally, fight the tendency to finish quickly. There is no correlation between those students who finish first and those who do the best on a test. Work until you are satisfied that you have answered all of the questions to the best of your ability. If you have time, reread the instructions to make sure you completed the test correctly.

Tips for Answering Essay and Short-Answer Questions

Essay questions are usually the hardest questions to answer because the teacher doesn't provide you with a choice of answers to jog your memory. If you keep the following six principles in mind when answering these questions, however, you will find them less troublesome:

1. Read the question slowly, underlining key words and phrases as you do. This will help you determine just what is being asked in the question and the type of answer the teacher wants. Pay attention to length restrictions.

2. Organize your answer before you write it, using the words and organization presented in the question. Outline the different points that you need to make, incorporating introductory and summary statements. This will prevent the answer from reading like a list of facts.

3. Start with general statements and support them with facts and examples, which will help the organization of your answer. Such a presentation will be appreciated by the professor, who will have spent much of their time wading through swamps of unorganized essay answers.

4. When you're sure of the answer, be concise and write only what is requested. When you need to fudge an answer, write as much as you can on all of the topics that you feel relate to the question. Hopefully, the teacher will find something of value in your answer to warrant some points. Always write something! You will not get any credit for questions left blank, but you may pick up a point or two for "educated guesses."

5. Be conscious of time restrictions. It's very easy when writing lengthy answers to lose track of time, so keep your watch on your arm or desk or check the clock periodically to remind you to budget your time. Note that most teachers won't let you have your smartphone on your desk during a test, even if you say it's just to check the time.

6. If you have time, review your work to make sure you have adequately answered the questions and have checked your grammar and spelling.

Tips for Answering Objective Questions

When given a choice, I would rather take an objective test any day. This is because the answer is usually provided for you in the question, and all you need to do is to match the information given with what's stored in the parietal lobes of your brain. Here are some strategies that can be helpful in answering multiple-choice, matching, and true-false questions.

1. Read the question slowly, then answer quickly. If you're in doubt, answer with your first impression. This allows your subconscious mind to play a role in answering questions.

2. Beware of universal statements. They are almost always wrong because in academics there are very few universal truths. These statements contain words like always, *never, no, none, all, every,* and *most.*

3. Use a notation system to keep track of your thinking during the test. I use T (true), PT (partly true), F (false), and PF (partly false) to indicate my impression of a statement. This helps me separate the different choices and decreases the need for backtracking. This system is also very helpful for questions that contain "all of the above" or "none of the above" alternatives. When you're not sure of an answer, consider only those you have marked with a T or PT. This will increase your odds of getting the answer right.

4. When you're unsure of an answer, try these strategies:
   - The most general alternative tends to be correct.
   - The longest option is often correct.
   - Repetition of the question in the answer often indicates the answer is true.
   - If two opposite options are offered, choose one of them.
   - Choose true instead of false, because negative alternatives are harder to write.
   - If the answer is a number, the correct alternative is often a middle value, so eliminate the highest and lowest options.

- In blind guessing, choose the same option throughout, usually B or C.

    Remember, these are only tips, not hard-and-fast rules. Your knowledge is your best guide.

5. Avoid looking for patterns of answers in true-false or multiple-choice questions. There is usually not an even distribution in the answer key.

6. Use the process of elimination for matching. Match those you know first. Then select the rest from a reduced set of options.

7. When solving a problem, work out your answer before looking at the possible options. This will eliminate bias in your work. Also, save tough problems until last, unless they have a disproportionately high amount of credit.

If you follow these strategies, you'll find your test scores increasing significantly. Remember, there is a skill in learning, but there is also skill in communicating what you know on tests.

OVERCOMING TEST ANXIETY

The best way to alleviate exam jitters is to be prepared. For most people, the level of anxiety before and during the exam correlates inversely with the amount of time spent and the efficiency of that time—the more time and efficiency, the less anxiety.

I have treated several patients who had severe anxiety and they performed far below their level of competence as a result of it. I was taught a simple hypnotic technique to counteract test anxiety by Donald Schafer, MD, of the University of California, Irvine. This technique has worked well for my patients and should work for you if you diligently follow these simple steps:

- First, close your eyes and concentrate on your breathing for a few minutes. Let it become slower, deeper, and more regular.

- Then imagine yourself, comfortable and relaxed, at the place where you usually study.
- After you do this, pick up a pen or pencil (whichever you will use on the test) and suggest to yourself that when you do this just as the test begins, you will feel as comfortable as you do sitting in your study chair at home, or wherever you study.
- Repeat this suggestion several times, and let it work for you on exams.

If this doesn't work for you during the test, try closing your eyes and taking three slow, deep breaths. Take a minute to try to imagine a relaxing scene like lying on the beach or sitting near a warm fire in winter. This method should have a relaxing effect on you. If anxiety is causing you to blank out on material you know, take a minute and do these relaxation exercises. This practice will often remove the block.

3 BRAIN-BASED TECHNIQUES TO CALM YOUR NERVES AND ENHANCE COGNITIVE FUNCTION BEFORE A TEST

Breathe: Whenever you feel tense or anxious about a big test, try this simple breathing exercise to help you relax. Deep breathing also increases oxygen to the brain, which decreases brain fog and increases focus—two things that will help you on your exam.

1. Take a deep breath.
2. Hold it for one to two seconds.
3. Slowly exhale for about five seconds.
4. Repeat 10 times to feel more relaxed.

Practice meditation or pray: Meditation and prayer—as little as five minutes a day—have been found to have a number of benefits that can benefit you in test-taking, including:

- soothing stress
- sharpening focus
- boosting moods
- improving memory
- enhancing overall prefrontal cortex (PFC) function[2]
- improving executive function[3]
- reducing feelings of anxiety, depression, and irritability

The Ultimate Brain-Based Therapy: Harness your senses: Your brain is influenced by the environment around you. Take control of your sensory inputs to get into a better "head space" before a test.

- **Sight:** Take a few moments to look at nature pictures[4] or images of fractals (never-ending, repeating patterns found in nature),[5] which have been found to reduce stress.
- **Sound:** Music can calm you down, help you focus, and give you a mood boost. Create a playlist that works for you and listen to it on the way to your test.
- **Touch:** Ask a friend to give you a hug. This simple act prompts your brain to release the feel-good neurotransmitter oxytocin, which causes a reduction in the stress hormones cortisol and norepinephrine.
- **Smell:** A variety of scents have been found to help calm nerves, including lavender oil (for anxiety[6] and mood[7]), rose oil,[8,9] and chamomile.[10]
- **Taste:** Foods flavored with cinnamon, mint, sage, saffron, or nutmeg have been shown to act as mood boosters.[11]

AFTER THE EXAM

After your test is graded and handed back to you, you have three responsibilities:

1. Go over the exam and note what questions you missed and why you missed them. This is a helpful, although painful, way to learn. Keep in mind what Oprah Winfrey has said about this: "Failure is a great teacher, and if you are open to it, every mistake has a lesson to offer."

2. If you have questions that are marked wrong and you disagree with the keyed answer, approach the professor with your challenge. Be prepared; teachers will often change answers for students, but only if they can persuasively defend their choice of another answer.

3. If you note that some of the questions are written in an ambiguous fashion, tactfully bring them to the teacher's attention. Most teachers welcome feedback and have no desire to claim omnipotence. This will help keep future students from being faced with the same poor test questions.

CHANGE YOUR BRAIN, CHANGE YOUR GRADES: PRESSURIZING YOUR CABIN

- Several weeks before the exam: Establish a study schedule, study in units, engage in periodic overall reviews, have a complete set of notes and a "big picture" fact sheet, and be sure to ask the instructor about the content of the test.
- Several days before the exam: Study with a partner, go to class, and cram for review, not first exposure. When you need to cram cold material, know your notes and chapter summaries and secure old exams if permissible.

- The day before the exam: Do an overall, quick review emphasizing your notes and "big picture" fact sheet.
- The day of the exam: Eat moderately, arrive for the test a few minutes early, stay away from congregations of students, and find a seat away from distractions.
- Test-taking generalizations: Quickly overview the test, read the instructions, answer the questions you know first, answer as you think the professor would, take questions at their face value, and fight the impulse to finish quickly.
- When answering essay questions: Read the questions slowly, organize your answers, work from general to specific, be concise when you know an answer and lengthy when you do not, always write something, be conscious of your time, and review your work.
- When answering objective questions: Read the question slowly, answer quickly, look for universal statements, use a notation system, use the odds for questions if you do not know the answer, and change answers for good reasons—otherwise, go with your first impression.
- Alleviate test anxiety by being prepared and utilizing relaxation techniques.
- After the exam has been graded: Review it to see why you missed certain questions, discuss disagreements with the professor from a standpoint of knowledge, and give the professor your impression of the test.

13

LETTING YOURSELF OUT

Writing and Speaking

In the spring of my junior year in college, I was required to write 12 papers, three of them term papers. My ethics class was assigned six papers, one due every two weeks. I remember being frustrated in that class because I would get my papers back from the professor without any of his personal comments on them—only the grade in the upper right-hand corner. I wanted to get feedback on my work, and after he returned my fourth paper with only the grade marked in the upper right-hand corner again, I began to wonder if he was reading them at all. So, in my fifth paper I inserted a phrase at the bottom of the fourth page in the middle of a paragraph that said, "If you are still reading this, I will buy you a milkshake." In the margin he wrote, "Make it chocolate." It was his only comment on the paper!

Writing is a skill that will serve you well not only in middle school, high school, and college, but also throughout your life. Being able to write well will open many doors for you professionally. In the same way, being able to speak well in public is a skill that many employers desire. This chapter is about letting yourself out in writing and speaking. These two skills are grouped together in this chapter because of the many similarities between writing a paper and writing a speech. At the end of the chapter, you'll find techniques for enhancing the delivery of speeches. There are many good books and resources on writing and speaking effectively, so this chapter will be limited to eight steps that I found helpful in my own academic career.

1. Schedule your time

Meeting deadlines is an essential part of everyone's life and especially important when writing papers or speeches. Many professors lower your grade for late papers or won't accept them at all after the due date. If your speech is not written in time for you to practice it, you'll feel very nervous when you present it. As soon as you get an assignment, prepare a reasonable schedule around the remaining seven steps in this chapter. You'll save yourself many hours of lost sleep the few nights before the assignments are due.

2. Choose a topic from the heart

When choosing a topic for a paper or speech, opt for something you're passionate about or something that interests you. This will make the process more enjoyable for you and will increase the likelihood that you'll expend the necessary effort to complete the task on time. It will also make it more enjoyable for the audience or reader because when you are passionate about something, it comes through in your work. If you're bored by the subject, everybody else will be bored, too. Even if your instructor assigns a topic, try to find a way to inject your personality into it to make it unique. Write with your heart involved.

Stay away from abstract subjects. In general, people want to read or hear about things that affect their daily lives, like how to get better grades while studying less.

Don't put extra pressure on yourself to find a topic that has never been written or spoken about previously. As King Solomon wrote in the Book of Ecclesiastes, "What has been will be again, what has been done will be done again; there is nothing new under the sun." (Eccles. 1:9) This is still a good principle to follow. Choose topics that are new to your audience or put a new spin on a familiar subject to make it more interesting, but be reasonable in your expectations.

3. Narrow it down

After you have selected a topic, make sure it is narrow enough to handle in the required numbers of words or minutes. If the topic is too broad— "The Definition of the Universe," "The Nature of Matter," or "The Development of Human Thought and Its Significance for the Twenty-First Century"—you'll spend the whole paper or speech on generalities and be unable to say anything specific or practical. If you're not sure if your topic is too broad, ask your instructor for guidance. The goal in writing and speaking is not a lengthy dissertation that barely scratches the surface of a topic, but rather an organized, tightly constructed idea, argument, or message.

4. Do adequate research

Researching your paper or speech can be profitable and time efficient, or it can be unproductive and stress-inducing. The first thing to do is zero in on the topic you have in mind. What is the overall message you want to convey? Once you've locked in on what you want to get across, hit the books and the internet to find research to support your angle. Make sure to use the most reputable sources, such as books by experts in the field, journal papers and studies, TED Talks, and newspaper and magazine articles.

When researching a topic, take voluminous notes. The more information you have in front of you when writing the paper or speech, the easier it will be to compile. Also, keep a bibliography on the sources you have used. This will save you time if you need to refer to them again or if your teacher asks where you got a certain fact.

TECH TIP FROM CHLOE AND ALIZÉ

Be aware that Wikipedia and articles shared on social media are not necessarily reliable sources. Always check the information with independent sources to verify accuracy.

5. Make an outline

After you've researched the topic and taken adequate notes, make an outline of the paper or speech. Start by putting your thesis statement at the top of the page. Below that, list the main points (aim for three to five items) that support your thesis statement. Label them with Roman numerals (I, II, III, IV, V). Then expand the outline from there by adding supporting ideas for each main point. By starting with the main concepts, you can easily see the "big picture" of how your paper or speech will flow. Then you can simply add the details.

If you put sufficient thought and effort into the outline, you won't have to spend time rewriting the paper if it turns out that you don't like the way it's organized. Also, if you paraphrase the information in your outline instead of copying it out of a book or the internet word for word, it will make writing the paper easier. This way, you can pull information right out of the outline and into your paper.

Having a detailed outline will decrease the time it takes to write the final paper or speech, because you will be less prone to writer's block. Your outline will serve as a road map to remind you where you have been, where you are, and where you are going.

6. Discuss your ideas

After you've made an outline, it's a good idea to discuss it with a friend or with your teacher. They can give you valuable ideas and feedback on it, and at this stage, it isn't difficult to do major revisions. Don't wait until after you have finished writing your paper or speech to have your work reviewed. At that late stage, it is not only more difficult and time-consuming to make changes, but it is also more disheartening and ego-deflating. Pick someone to review your work who believes in you and whom you trust with your feelings. You'll be more likely to believe and accept any constructive criticism they might give you.

7. Write a first draft

Writing the first draft of the paper or speech is actually the easiest part of the process if you have chosen an interesting topic, have kept its scope narrow, have sufficiently researched and outlined it, and have discussed it with someone you respect.

A simple rule to follow in writing or speaking is to first tell your audience what you plan to say, then say it, and then recap what you have just said. This will give the material an organized appearance, and it will also reinforce the major points.

When writing, try to keep in mind five simple concepts:

- Say only one thing at a time and keep the arguments, examples, and contributory ideas pertinent to the topic.
- Ensure that the sentences have continuity and that the ideas flow comfortably together.
- Be as clear as possible. If you wish to make a point, be certain you have made it. Clear writing indicates clear thinking.
- Don't use extra words or examples. Be as concise as possible to promote clarity. Take out or restructure any sentences or words that clutter the paper.
- Have some fun with it. If a point can be made in a funny or humorous way, it has a better chance of being remembered, and it will also keep the audience's attention focused on the paper or the speech. This is especially useful when the information gets complicated or dense.

When writing the first draft, let the ideas flow onto the paper. Don't edit your work or make revisions as you go. You will have time later to correct the grammar and punctuation. Just get the ideas onto the paper for the first writing. Some people spend so much time trying to perfect their writing as they go that they never get past the first paragraph!

8. Revise your work

As any professional writer will say, "writing is rewriting." Don't expect your first draft to be your final draft. In fact, revising your paper or speech can be just as time-consuming as writing the initial draft. This is the time to improve sentence structure, choose stronger vocabulary, and correct punctuation, as well as ensure that the ideas flow in a logical sequence. This is usually not as interesting as writing the first draft, but if proper time is taken, the paper or speech will take on a professional appearance, and the mechanics will not distract from the information you are trying to convey.

TIPS FOR SPEAKING IN PUBLIC

After a paper is finished, you turn it in and hope for a good grade, but after you've finished writing a speech, your work is only half over. The most nerve-racking part for many is to get up in front of a group of people and share their speech. I know this is true, because I used to get the feeling of having a herd of angry mosquitoes (most people get butterflies—I get mosquitoes) in the pit of my stomach as I was about to deliver a speech. Also, at the beginning of my speech, my voice would betray me and would sound as though someone was letting the air out of a balloon slowly while stretching the opening of it, creating a painful, squeaky noise.

By participating on two college speech teams and acting as the president of the second one, I learned the following helpful strategies to overcome my fear of public speaking and deliver a winning speech:

- *Pick a topic you love.* As mentioned earlier, be sure to choose a topic familiar to you and/or very interesting to you. If you're excited by the material, you're more likely to get the audience excited about it too.

- *Revise the script until you've got it just right.* If you feel good about what you are going to present, you'll feel confident about delivering it.

- *Perform your speech in front of friends or the mirror, or use your phone to record yourself.* This gives you the advantage of presenting the speech to a friendly audience—even if it's just yourself—that can provide feedback. If you know how you look as you are presenting the speech, you can adjust your posturing and gestures until you feel comfortable. Take note of your timing and voice level too. For example, pausing a few seconds before a major point is a great way to indicate to the audience that you're about to share something very important. And practice making good eye contact with the audience. If your image in the mirror walks away or falls asleep, you know you're in trouble.

- *Time yourself.* If your speech is supposed to be 10 minutes and the material you've written only comes to three minutes or goes on for 25 minutes, you're going to have a big problem. Use the stopwatch on your phone to make sure you can deliver the speech in the assigned time limit.

- *Practice, practice, practice!* The more familiar you are with the subject, the less chance you will feel overwhelmed by nerves. Even though you wrote the speech, you need to review it as much as possible, so if you do start to panic, you won't blank on its contents. Just like the test-taking tip you saw in an earlier chapter: Trust yourself.

- *Keep a cheat sheet.* Carry notes with you even if you are delivering your speech from memory. This will give you the added assurance that if you completely blank out on your presentation, you can quickly find your place and proceed. But use the notes only if you really can't remember anything. If you're too focused on the notes, you're likely to block the information that you need. And no audience wants to watch someone deliver a speech with their head down and their nose in their notes.

- *To memorize a speech, keep the outline uppermost in your mind.* The "big picture" is very helpful here. If you know where you have been in your speech, where you are, and where you are going, you might block out a few words, but you can always move to the next major point.

- *Be enthusiastic!* Realize that you're developing a tool that can make you feel better about yourself. If you can write or speak well, you have a powerful vehicle for sharing your ideas with others. This is healthy from a psychological and social standpoint, because as you learn to communicate better with others, you'll have the opportunity to be involved in more human interactions, and these will be more satisfying.

4 STEPS TO SOOTHE PUBLIC SPEAKING ANXIETY

Throughout my career, I've appeared on TV hundreds of times, and I really enjoy having the opportunity to share what we've learned from our brain imaging work with the audience. But I wasn't always a natural in front of the camera. In fact, I still vividly remember my very first TV interview for CNN in 1989. They wanted to interview me about an article I had written for *Parade* magazine called "How to Get Out of Your Own Way." It had struck a chord with readers and gotten a huge response. But just before I was about to go on air, I became racked with anxiety. My heart started beating out of control, and I felt as though I couldn't catch my breath. I wanted to run from the studio. Luckily, as a psychiatrist, I treat people with anxiety, so I followed the same four steps I give to my patients.

1. *Slow down your breathing.* When you take shallow, fast breaths, your brain gets less oxygen. And anything that reduces oxygen to the brain can trigger feelings of anxiety, fear, and panic.
2. *Don't leave.* Running away from the situation won't solve the problem. In my example, if I had left the CNN studio that day, I probably never would have agreed to do a TV interview again.

3. *Write down your thoughts.* You will learn much more about this in the following chapter, but basically, if you write down what you are thinking, you can challenge unfounded, fearful thoughts. In my case, I was afraid I would stutter and look stupid. But I had never stuttered in my life, so it was very unlikely I would start then.

4. *Take calming supplements or medications, if needed.* If the first three steps don't help, you may want to consider this final step.

CHANGE YOUR BRAIN, CHANGE YOUR GRADES: LETTING YOURSELF OUT

- Writing and speaking well will serve you all of your life.
- In writing papers or speeches, follow eight steps: prepare a reasonable time schedule, choose a topic interesting to you, narrow the topic, research your presentation, outline your work, discuss the outline with a professor or friend, write a first draft, then revise your work.
- Tell the audience what you plan to say, say it, and then review what you said.
- When writing, keep five concepts in mind: say one thing at a time, write with continuity, be as clear as possible, be concise, and use humor, when appropriate.
- When speaking, be interested in your topic; have a well-written speech; perform the speech in front of friends or mirror; practice, practice, practice; time yourself; carry notes with you; and memorize the outline of the speech first.
- Be enthusiastic! The more you write or speak, the more you will improve and the easier it will be.

14

KILLING THE ANTs

How to Feel Good Every Day

Don't believe every stupid thought in your head. Did you know that your thoughts can lie? And that they lie a lot? Your thoughts can make you feel sad, insecure, and incapable, and they can get in the way of your success in school. Take Marcus, for example. He came to see me because he was having a lot of trouble with his schoolwork. In his first session with me, he told me:

"I'm an idiot."

"My teachers hate me."

"I can never be as good as other kids."

I call these thoughts ANTs, or automatic negative thoughts. I taught Marcus seven simple strategies to gain control of his thinking, calm his mind, and focus his attention so he could achieve the success in school he wanted. You can learn from them too.

1. YOUR THOUGHTS DIRECTLY AFFECT HOW YOU FEEL

Every time you have a thought, your brain releases chemicals that impact the way you feel. Whenever you have a sad thought, a mad thought, or a hopeless thought, such as "I'm an idiot," your brain releases chemicals that make you feel bad. Conversely, every time you have a happy

YOUR BRAIN IS HARDWIRED
FOR NEGATIVE THINKING

For our cave-dwelling human ancestors, negative thinking was a powerful tool in our survival arsenal. Focusing on the negative helped us avoid getting eaten by a saber-toothed tiger or falling off a cliff to our death. Being acutely aware of the potential dangers in life is part of why humans have survived so long. As our society has evolved, however, we are no longer under constant threat from wild animals or unknown terrain. But the human brain hasn't evolved as quickly as our surroundings. In fact, research shows that our brains are still more attuned to negative experiences than positive ones.[1] Just look at the news we consume—it's one disaster after another. We're far more likely to seek out negative news. In one study, people were 63 percent more likely to click on headlines with negative adjectives than those with positive wording.[2] The good news is that you can train your brain to flip this natural tendency upside down and swap out negative, unhelpful thinking for positive thoughts that help you achieve your goals.

thought, a loving thought, or a hopeful thought, your brain releases chemicals that make you feel good immediately. Thinking too many bad thoughts can make you feel bad—about yourself, about your ability to do your schoolwork, about your teachers, about everything—and can prevent you from achieving your goals.

2. ASK YOURSELF IF YOUR THOUGHTS ARE TRUE

Learn how to question the thoughts that prevent you from being the student you want to be. My good friend Byron Katie created an exercise called "The Work" that can help turn around negative thoughts and beliefs that fuel anxiety and depression. Basically, any time you have a negative, hurtful, distressing thought, ask yourself if it is true. For example, if you think "I'm terrible at history," ask yourself if it is true. Are you really terrible at it, or do you just need to study harder? Or do you need to find ways to make the subject more interesting to you so you will want to learn it? When you see the truth of your thoughts, you can take better control of your mind. What a comfort!

3. MEET THE 7 TYPES OF ANTs

Before you can kill the ANTs, you need to learn how to identify them. There are seven different types of ANT species:

- **All-or-Nothing ANTs.** These ANTs think in absolutes—things are all good or all bad—and use words like *all, always, never, none, nothing, no one, everyone,* and *every time.*

CAN YOU THINK YOUR WAY TO A BETTER BRAIN?

I once did a study on negative thinking versus positive thinking with psychologist Noelle Nelson, the author of *The Power of Appreciation.* We performed two SPECT scans on her brain under very different conditions. For one of the scans, she spent 30 minutes contemplating all the wonderful things in her life that made her feel grateful. After these positive thoughts, her SPECT brain scans showed very healthy blood flow and activity. For the other scan, I asked Noelle to spend 30 minutes thinking about all of her worst fears and worries. Her negative brain showed marked differences compared with her positive brain. Her negative brain showed lowered activity in two important regions, the cerebellum and temporal lobes. As you recall, the cerebellum is involved in processing complex information, and low activity in this area is associated with poor learning, slowed thinking, and disorganization. Low activity in the temporal lobes can cause problems with memory and moods. Noelle's story shows that negative thinking leads to negative changes in the brain that can undermine your efforts in school. On the other hand, positive thinking boosts your brainpower for better performance.

- **Just the Bad ANTs.** This ANT can't see anything good! It sees only the bad side of any situation.
- **Guilt-Beating ANTs.** These ANTs think in words like *should, must, ought to,* or *have to* that are actually demotivating.
- **Labeling ANTs.** Attaching negative labels to yourself or someone else strengthens negative pathways in the brain and keeps you stuck in your old ways.
- **Fortune-Teller ANTs.** Don't listen to this lying ANT! Fortune-teller ANTs predict the worst possible outcome with little or no evidence.
- **Mind Reader ANTs.** This ANT thinks it can see inside someone else's mind. It thinks it knows how others think and feel without even being told.
- **Blaming ANTs.** Blaming others for your problems makes you a victim and prevents you from admitting your mistakes or learning from them.

4. KILL THE ANTs

To kill the ANTs, you need to identify the species, then reframe the thought with honest, rational thinking. Here are examples:

ANT	Species	Kill the ANT
I never do well on essay tests.	All or Nothing	That's not true. I usually do well, but I missed the mark on this one. I'll learn from my mistakes on this one and do better next time.
I only got a 90 out of 100 on the exam. I'm worthless.	Just the Bad	Getting a 90 is a great accomplishment, and I should be proud.

I should work on the outline for my term paper, but I don't want to.	Guilt Beating	I want to finish my term paper this weekend because it's important to me, and completing the outline will help me do it.
I'm a lousy student.	Labeling	If I stay focused and study really hard, I can get good grades.
The other students are going to hate my speech.	Fortune-Teller	I can't predict this without having proof.
My study partner must be mad at me because she didn't reply to my text right away.	Mind Reader	I don't know that for sure. Maybe she's just busy studying for another class. I'll speak to her about it.
It's my teacher's fault I didn't get a better grade.	Blaming	I need to look at my part in the problem and figure out what I can do better next time.

5. TAKE A BREAK TO PREVENT BURNOUT

For students, there's so much pressure to succeed, it can leave you feeling overwhelmed and stressed out. I know from personal experience what it feels like to be burned out—when you've been working for so many hours that you can't think straight anymore . . . *and you still have more work to do.* Here are some tips to help you avoid getting caught up in a pressure cooker.

- *Accept your limitations and know when enough is enough.* Learn to be okay with not being able to be superhuman, and don't expect perfection from yourself. It's bad enough that your teachers are putting a lot of pressure on you; don't make it worse by putting added pressure on yourself.

- *Try to step back, take a break, and relax.* Your best work is done when you're well rested and relaxed. In fact, too much stress releases chemicals in your brain that reduce your

TECH TIP FROM CHLOE AND ALIZÉ
Remember to put "me time" in your schedule and set an alert as a reminder to power down and give your brain and body a rest.

cognitive performance and lower your ability to problem-solve. I know it can be hard to take a break, but your best really requires rest. Remind yourself that this is not an excuse to procrastinate or not do work but permission to prevent burnout.

- *Schedule breaks.* Time management is a very important factor in avoiding burnout. Figure out what things you want to make time for and put them in your schedule.

6. SPREAD KINDNESS TO YOUR TEACHERS

One thing I have found that makes school so much better is befriending your teachers. Whether you like it or not, you're going to see these people on a regular basis, so why not make it a more pleasant experience? It takes simple things like being respectful in class, having a positive attitude, and telling your instructor when you appreciate something about their teaching style. One very important thing to keep in mind is to avoid overdoing it. Teachers have seen it all before—the "kiss-ups," the ones who bring them chocolate, and the ones who say, "My mom's the head of the PTA, now give me that A." Your teachers can see through any phony attempts to be BFFs with them. It could backfire and work against you. On the other hand, you might actually end up liking them and getting even more out of the relationship.

CHANGE YOUR BRAIN, CHANGE YOUR GRADES: KILLING THE ANTs

- Your thoughts directly affect how you feel. Bad thoughts make you feel bad; good thoughts make you feel good.
- Question the veracity of the thoughts in your head: Ask yourself if they are true.
- Meet the seven types of ANTs. These automatic negative thoughts can make you feel bad and keep you from achieving your goals.
- Kill the ANTs. Learn how to reframe ANTs so they don't get in the way of your success as a student.
- Take a break to prevent burnout. Give yourself some "me time" to keep your brain and body refreshed and relaxed for better performance.
- Spread kindness to your teachers. Make your time in school more enjoyable by developing a positive relationship with your instructors.

15

WRAPPING THE PRESENT

GETTING THE BEST OUT OF YOURSELF

This book is designed to be a gift that keeps on giving. The gift's contents include better grades, more comprehensive knowledge, and more effective use of your time. But the results are up to you! If you use this gift—practicing the principles described and approaching your studies with an enthusiastic attitude—you'll be very satisfied with it. However, if you neglect to use your gift—sticking with old, unproductive habits and patterns or giving up on your goals when the going gets tough—you'll be setting yourself up for disappointment.

Realize at the outset that you are primarily responsible for your success. Don't fall victim to the Blaming ANT by blaming others or circumstances for your failures. This is a dangerous habit, because you're admitting to a loss of control over your life. And if you're not in control of yourself, who will be?

This final chapter is intended to finish the wrapping of your present by placing a splendid bow on it. The end of this book will show you that developing your "other sides," sowing healthy seeds, and directing your pain will strengthen your overall abilities as a student and as a person.

Everyone realizes there is more to life than just being a student, but if you aren't careful, you'll find yourself engaged only in studying or activities related to studying. When this happens, you'll forfeit the necessary education offered by the other areas of your life. Decide at the outset what place studies will have in your world, but don't let them dominate you. You'll have a more well-rounded education if you take care of your body, establish solid relationships, and cultivate outside interests.

1. Take care of your physical side

Be extremely attentive to your physical health. Your body is the instrument of learning, and it must be finely tuned. There are many studies suggesting that regular exercise augments your mental stamina, memory, attention, problem solving, planning, and organizing, and even enhances feelings of self-confidence. Exercise also increases production of endorphins in your body, natural chemicals that add to your sense of well-being. In addition, understand that being overweight will cause your body to divert energy from your brain cells to feed your fat cells. Your ideal body weight is also your peak brainpower weight.

Feed your body a balanced diet to operate at peak efficiency. To fuel your brain and body for better performance, follow these nine rules for brain-healthy eating.

- *Rule #1: Focus on high-quality calories.* The quality of your food matters much more than the quantity. Compare a 500-calorie cinnamon roll to a 500-calorie plate of salmon, spinach, red bell peppers, blueberries, and walnuts. One will drain your energy and increase inflammation; the other will supercharge your mind and keep your body healthy.
- *Rule #2: Drink plenty of water.* Your brain is 80 percent water. Staying hydrated helps optimize the brain's power. Being dehydrated by just 2 percent impairs performance in tasks that require attention, immediate memory skills, and physical performance.
- *Rule #3: Eat high-quality protein in small doses throughout the day.* Consuming protein helps stave off hunger and prevents energy crashes.
- *Rule #4: Eat smart carbohydrates.* Carbs that are low glycemic and high in fiber—think vegetables and fruits like blueberries, pears, and apples—stabilize blood sugar and provide sustained energy.

- *Rule #5: Focus your diet on healthy fats.* Did you know that 60 percent of the solid weight of your brain is fat? Good fats are essential to your health. Choose healthy fats like avocados, fish (wild salmon, trout, sea bass), nuts and seeds, olives, olive oil, and coconut oil.
- *Rule #6: Eat from the rainbow.* Include natural foods in your diet that reflect the color of the spectrum, such as blueberries, pomegranates, yellow squash, and red bell peppers. This will boost the power-packed flavonoids to elevate antioxidant levels in your body and help keep your brain young.
- *Rule #7: Cook with brain-healthy herbs and spices.* Herbs and spices—including ginger, garlic, oregano, cinnamon, turmeric, and thyme—contain many health-promoting substances and add flavor to your food.
- *Rule #8: Make sure your food is as clean as possible.* Whenever you can, eat organically grown or raised foods, as pesticides, hormones, and antibiotics used in the food industry can accumulate in your brain and body and cause problems.
- *Rule #9: If you struggle with any mental health or physical issues, eliminate any potential allergens or internal attackers.* People often feel and perform better when they go on an elimination diet that gets rid of wheat (and all food containing gluten), dairy, corn, soy, processed foods, all forms of sugar and sugar alternatives, and food dyes and additives.

2. Develop your relational side

Much satisfaction and fulfillment in life comes from your relationships with other people. If you neglect this aspect of your life because of your studies, then you are cheating yourself. Valuable, practical lessons are learned from these encounters, and it is to your advantage to cultivate the relationships that are important to you.

Using your studies as a way to avoid meaningful associations will perhaps lessen your pain in life, because relationships can often be painful. However, few people reach their full potential as humans without significant personal relationships. As I mentioned in the first chapter, there is no growth or success without some pain and risk-taking. We are all relational beings; don't let your studies cheat you out of being human.

3. Cultivate your interests outside of school

Many careers are born not from formal education, but from hobbies or extracurricular activities, like photography, journalism, sports, or student government. Engaging in these outlets will help you develop areas of your life that are often not challenged in teaching institutions. Also, these activities may give you an added bonus of becoming a more interesting person.

One hobby that I had in high school and part of college was raising my raccoon, Hermie. Hermie taught me many invaluable lessons. First, she taught me the art of diplomacy. One time I came home and found my mother and Hermie in a major skirmish. It seemed Hermie decided that it would be great fun to TP my mother's bathroom, turn on all the faucets, and play in the toilet bowl. In addition, she continually flushed the toilet—lowering the water pressure in the neighborhood. When my dad got home, my mother declared that it was either her or the raccoon, that they both could not live in the same house! Dad did not help matters by hesitating before he answered her! Believe me, I had to make major concessions to keep Hermie from getting the boot.

In college, I became known as the guy with the raccoon, and all the other students wanted to meet Hermie. It turned out to be a great way to meet new people and make friends I probably never would have encountered if it weren't for Hermie.

Developing your "other sides" is about learning how to become a whole person. By taking care of your body, establishing nurturing relationships, and cultivating your outside interests, you'll be enhancing your total education. Never forget that you're much more than a student! A major purpose of this book is to help you become a more efficient student, so you'll have more time to develop other, equally important aspects of your life. This is the pretty bow on the present!

SOWING SEEDS

Jesus told this parable: "A farmer went out to sow his seed. As he was scattering the seed, some fell along the path; it was trampled on, and the birds of the air ate it up. Some fell on rock, and when it came up, the plants withered because they had no moisture. Other seed fell among thorns, which grew up with it and choked the plants. Still other seed fell on good soil. It came up and yielded a crop, a hundred times more than was sown." (Luke 8:5–8)

Time and effort (seeds) are not the deciding factors for your school performance. You all know many students who study constantly yet have no grasp of the information or do poorly on their exams. Conversely, you know students who get As in their classes, regardless of the amount of sleep they get or how many breaks they take. The yield of the harvest from your studies will depend upon the quality of the seeds and the way they are planted. Reviewing the major points of this book—basically, getting the big picture of *Change Your Brain, Change Your Grades*—will help you to cultivate the soil of your mind.

- Having a balanced lifestyle is important for everything you do in life. Many things go into performing well in even just one thing. Sleep, exercise, and energy can make a huge difference in your grade on an exam. Keeping a balanced lifestyle, to the best of your ability, will always increase your chances of success.
- Changing bad study habits and patterns requires being motivated to change, actually deciding to change, having the right attitude and tools for change, persevering to entrench new ways, and setting yourself up to win.
- Preparation is paramount to accomplishment. Start at the beginning of the beginning to lay a solid foundation of knowledge.
- Study with a purpose. Know what you want to accomplish, what you have studied, and what still remains to be learned.
- The big picture is what you will remember, and it is your key to understanding the details.

- Start with generalities and work toward specifics.
- Develop the discipline of organizing your time, your resources, and—most of all—yourself. Use a systematic approach to your classes and be realistic in the time and energy you plan to devote to them.
- Utilize the resources available to you. Read the syllabus and foundational material in your texts. Obtain review books and old tests. Glean all you can from your teachers and other students.
- Approach your classes with a conscientious attitude in the beginning of the course, planning to do your best to establish a foundation and enhance self-confidence. Know your goals going in, as this will keep you from getting discouraged.
- Try different study methods to see what works best for you in different situations. Study in defined units with frequent review, and always try to apply what you are learning.
- Go to class—it is the basic tool of education. In order to profit the most from lectures, be prepared for them by reading ahead to give yourself more familiarity with the material.
- Listening in class involves hearing, processing, acknowledging, reacting to, and assimilating the material. Active listening is necessary if you are to assimilate the subject matter.
- When taking notes, take your cues from the lecturer. Remember, notes are the basis for most exams—a good set of notes is imperative! Rewrite them after class in order to get more exposure to them.
- Memory succeeds with associations. Understand the material before you attempt to memorize it. Become skilled with the use of memory aids to develop associations.
- Learn to study with a partner. This practice will break the monotony of studying, help you clarify questionable areas, and give you another perspective on the important points when it's time to review for exams.
- Prepare for exams by budgeting your study time, studying in units, and engaging in periodic overall reviews. Ensure that you

have a complete set of lecture notes, made-up test questions, and a "big picture" fact sheet.

- Find out as much as you can about the exam beforehand. Utilize old tests (if permissible) to see how the professor asks questions and what material they have deemed important in the past.
- Cram for review, not just exposure. Recentness of exposure is the limiting factor for short-term memory.
- During the exam, read the instructions carefully, answer the questions that you know first, take questions at their face value, and fight the tendency to finish quickly.
- Learn from exams by reviewing them afterward and questioning the professor if you disagree with them.
- When writing a paper or a speech, schedule your time, choose a narrow topic, research it well, make an outline, discuss your ideas, and then write and revise your work.
- Keys to becoming an effective speaker involve believing in your topic, writing a good speech, practicing it, and delivering it with enthusiasm.
- Develop the other areas of your life—your education in life involves much more than any school can offer.

The final method of planting seeds for your education is that of helping other students. When you excel in a class, be willing to tutor those who are struggling in it. I have spent many hours tutoring other students, and the harvest I have reaped for my efforts was invariably greater than that sown. Every time you teach something, it helps engrave that information deeper into your parietal lobe. For one neuroanatomy midterm exam, I spent over 15 hours working with two students who were having trouble in the class. When it was over, I not only had the satisfaction of knowing I had helped two friends pass a tough exam, but I also had the pleasure of writing a perfect exam for myself. You will reap what you sow, so use your talent and resources in the most productive ways possible.

Appendix A

107 BRIGHT MINDS WAYS TO GROW YOUR BRAIN

B is for Blood Flow

1. Drink plenty of water—blood is mostly water!
2. Limit caffeine and eliminate nicotine.
3. Take up a racquet sport.
4. Enjoy a small piece of sugar-free dark chocolate.
5. Supplement with ginkgo biloba.
6. Spice up your food by adding cayenne pepper.
7. Eat arginine-rich foods, such as beets.
8. Eat magnesium-rich food, such as pumpkin seeds.
9. Drink green tea.
10. Know your blood pressure and keep it healthy. (About 4 percent of Americans ages 12 to 19 have hypertension and another 10 percent have elevated blood pressure.[1])

R is for Rational Thinking

1. Start every day with "Today is going to be a great day."
2. Finish every day by writing down "What went well today."
3. Write down three things you're grateful for every day.
4. Challenge any negative thoughts.
5. Kill the ANTs (automatic negative thoughts).
6. Show your appreciation by letting people know you care about them.

7. Practice meditation.
8. When things don't go your way, look for the positive spin.
9. Be as kind to yourself as you are to other people.
10. Think of something wonderful and notice how it makes you feel (where you bring your attention determines how you feel).

I is for Inflammation

1. Floss daily and care for your gums.
2. Test your C-reactive protein levels (aim for under 1.0 mg/L) and omega-3 index (aim for >8%).
3. Eliminate any trans fats from your diet.
4. Limit omega-6 rich foods, such as corn, soy, and processed foods.
5. Increase omega-3 rich foods, such as fish and avocados.
6. Take omega-3 supplements.
7. Take curcumin supplements.
8. Take vitamin B_6, B_{12}, and folate supplements.
9. Eat prebiotic foods, such as asparagus, onions, garlic, and apples.
10. Add probiotic foods and/or supplements to your diet.

G is for Genetics

1. If you have family members with mental health challenges or memory problems, you need to get serious about your own brain health as soon as possible by following these BRIGHT MINDS tips.
2. Consider genetic testing to identify any vulnerabilities.
3. Believe that your behavior can turn on or off many "troublemaker genes."
4. Limit high-glycemic, saturated-fat foods, such as pizza, processed cheeses, and microwave popcorn.
5. Practice stress-relief techniques.
6. Avoid self-medicating with alcohol, drugs, or cigarettes.

7. Work on addressing past emotional trauma.
8. Eat blueberries.

H is for Head Trauma

1. Do not text while walking or driving.
2. Wear a seatbelt.
3. Be thoughtful about your actions.
4. Wear a helmet when skiing, biking, etc.
5. Avoid climbing ladders.
6. Slow down.
7. Hold the handrail when going down the stairs.
8. If you've had head trauma, check your hormones.
9. Do not wear headphones while walking.
10. Consider trying hyperbaric oxygen therapy.

T is for Toxins

1. Decrease exposure by buying organic when possible.
2. Avoid fumes when pumping gas.
3. Quit smoking and avoid secondhand smoke.
4. Support your kidneys by drinking more water.
5. Support your liver by limiting alcohol and eating brassicas (broccoli, cauliflower, Brussels sprouts, cabbage, etc.).
6. Support your gut by eating more fiber.
7. Support your skin by sweating from exercise and saunas.
8. Check your home for mold if you suspect a problem.
9. Don't drink or eat out of plastic containers.
10. Use the Think Dirty app to identify personal care products that contain toxins.

M is for Mental Health

1. Engage in regular physical exercise to boost dopamine and serotonin levels.

2. If you are a worrier, consider serotonin-boosting 5-HTP.
3. If you have trouble with focus, consider a higher-protein, lower-carbohydrate diet.
4. Eat up to eight fruits and vegetables a day—there is a linear correlation with happiness!
5. Practice meditation.
6. Take a walk in nature.
7. Practice ANT therapy (see chapter 14).
8. Know and optimize your vitamin D levels.
9. Add saffron to your meals to help mood and memory.
10. If natural interventions prove ineffective, consult a mental health professional.

I is for Immunity/Infections

1. If you are struggling with mental health issues that do not get better with standard treatments, consider being tested for exposure to infections.
2. Decrease alcohol intake. (Why do nurses swab alcohol on your skin before giving you a shot? To decrease the bacteria. Drinking excessive alcohol can upset the gut microbiome, which is critical to immunity.)
3. Try an elimination diet for one month to see if food allergies may be damaging your immune system (eliminate gluten, dairy, corn, and soy to start).
4. Avoid hiking where deer ticks live.
5. Know and optimize your vitamin D levels.
6. Add extra vitamin C to your diet.
7. Supplement with aged garlic.
8. Add onions to your diet.
9. Add shiitake mushrooms to your diet.
10. Watch a comedy—research shows laughter can boost immunity.[2,3,4]

N is for Neurohormone Issues

1. If you are struggling with brain fog, fatigue, and/or chronic stress, check your hormone levels, especially the thyroid.
2. Avoid hormone disruptors, such as BPAs, phthalates, parabens, and pesticides in products.
3. Avoid animal proteins raised with hormones and antibiotics.
4. Add fiber to your diet to decrease unhealthy estrogens in the body.
5. Lift weights to boost testosterone.
6. Limit sugar, which disrupts hormones.
7. Supplement with zinc to help boost testosterone.
8. Take cortisol-reducing supplements, such as ashwagandha (also supports the thyroid).
9. If you have an underactive thyroid, use hormone replacement as needed.

D is for Diabesity

1. Know your BMI (body mass index) and check it monthly.
2. Don't drink your calories—be aware that sugar-sweetened sodas and juices as well as high-calorie cocktails can add up to weight gain.
3. Go for the highest-quality calories you can find, and not too many of them if you need to lose weight.
4. Eat from the rainbow, with a goal of eating foods of many different natural colors (not Skittles).
5. Have protein and healthy fat at each meal to stabilize blood sugar and cravings.
6. Eat "smart carbs"—those that are low glycemic and high in fiber.
7. Read food labels—if you don't know what's in something, don't eat it.
8. If you are overweight, develop lifelong habits to lose weight gradually rather than crash dieting.

9. Add cinnamon and nutmeg to your meals to help balance blood sugar levels.
10. Only love foods that love you back.

S is for Sleep

1. If you snore, get assessed for sleep apnea.
2. Eliminate caffeine.
3. Put blue light blockers on your electronic gadgets.
4. Cool your home a bit before bedtime.
5. Darken your room at night.
6. Turn off all gadgets at night.
7. Maintain a regular sleep schedule.
8. Supplement with melatonin and magnesium.
9. Listen to a hypnosis audio program or app.
10. If you are a worrier, try 5-HTP.

Appendix B

AMEN CLINIC LEARNING DISABILITY SCREENING QUESTIONNAIRE

Please rate yourself on each of the symptoms listed below using the following scale. If possible, to provide the most complete picture, have another person (such as a parent) rate you as well.

0—Never
1—Rarely
2—Occasionally
3—Frequently
4—Very Frequently
NA—Not Applicable/Not Known

Reading

Other Self

___   ___ 1. I am a poor reader.
___   ___ 2. I do not like reading.
___   ___ 3. I make mistakes when reading, like skipping words or lines.
___   ___ 4. I have to read the same line twice.
___   ___ 5. I have problems remembering what I read even though I have read all the words.

___ ___ 6. I reverse letters when I read (such as b/d or p/q).

___ ___ 7. I switch letters in words when reading (such as god and dog).

___ ___ 8. My eyes hurt or water when I read.

___ ___ 9. Words tend to blur when I read.

___ ___ 10. Words tend to move around the page when I read.

___ ___ 11. When reading, I have difficulty understanding main ideas or important details.

Writing

___ ___ 12. I have messy handwriting.

___ ___ 13. My work tends to be messy.

___ ___ 14. I prefer printing rather than writing in cursive.

___ ___ 15. My letters run into each other or there is no space between words.

___ ___ 16. I have trouble staying within the lines.

___ ___ 17. I have problems with grammar or punctuation.

___ ___ 18. I am a poor speller.

___ ___ 19. I have trouble copying off the board or from a page in a book.

___ ___ 20. I have trouble getting thoughts from my brain to the paper.

___ ___ 21. I can tell a story but cannot write it.

Body Awareness/Spatial Relationships

___ ___ 22. I have trouble knowing my left from my right.

___ ___ 23. I have trouble keeping things within columns or coloring within the lines.

___ ___ 24. I tend to be clumsy and uncoordinated.

___ ___ 25. I have difficulty with eye-hand coordination.

___ ___ 26. I have difficulty with concepts such as up, down, over, or under.

___ ___ 27. I tend to bump into things when walking.

Oral Expressive Language

___ ___ 28. I have difficulty expressing myself in words.

___ ___ 29. I have trouble finding the right words to say in conversations.

___ ___ 30. I have trouble talking about a subject or getting to the point in conversations.

Receptive Language

___ ___ 31. I have trouble keeping up or understanding what is being said in conversations.

___ ___ 32. I tend to misunderstand people and give the wrong answers in conversations.

___ ___ 33. I have trouble understanding directions people tell me.

___ ___ 34. I have trouble telling the direction a sound is coming from.

___ ___ 35. I have trouble filtering out background noises.

Math

___ ___ 36. I am poor at basic math skills for my age (adding, subtracting, multiplying, and dividing)

___ ___ 37. I make careless mistakes in math.

___ ___ 38. I tend to switch numbers around.

___ ___ 39. I have difficulty with word problems.

Sequencing

___ ___ 40. I have trouble getting everything in the right order when I speak.

___ ___ 41. I have trouble telling time.

___ ___ 42. I have trouble with alphabetical order.

___ ___ 43. I have trouble saying the months of the year in order.

Abstraction

____ ____ 44. I have trouble understanding jokes people tell me.

____ ____ 45. I tend to take things too literally.

Organization

____ ____ 46. My paperwork is messy or disorganized.

____ ____ 47. My room is messy.

____ ____ 48. I tend to shove everything into my backpack, desk, or closet.

____ ____ 49. I have multiple piles around my room.

____ ____ 50. I have trouble planning my time.

____ ____ 51. I am frequently late or in a hurry.

____ ____ 52. I often do not write down assignments or tasks and end up forgetting what to do.

Memory

____ ____ 53. I have trouble with my memory.

____ ____ 54. I remember things from long ago but not recent events.

____ ____ 55. It is hard for me to memorize things for school or work.

____ ____ 56. I know something one day but do not remember it the next.

____ ____ 57. I forget what I am going to say right in the middle of saying it.

____ ____ 58. I have trouble following directions that have more than one or two steps.

Social Skills

____ ____ 59. I have few or no friends.

____ ____ 60. I have trouble reading body language or facial expressions of others.

____ ____ 61. My feelings are often or easily hurt.

____ ____ 62. I tend to get into trouble with friends, teachers, parents, or bosses.

____ ____ 63. I feel uncomfortable around people I do not know well.

____ ____ 64. I am teased by others.

____ ____ 65. Friends do not ask me to do things with them.

____ ____ 66. I do not get together with others outside of school or work.

Irlen Syndrome (see Irlen.com for more information)

____ ____ 67. I am light sensitive (bothered by glare, sunlight, headlights, or streetlights).

____ ____ 68. I become tired, experience headaches or mood changes, and/or feel restless or inable to stay focused with bright or fluorescent lights.

____ ____ 69. I have trouble reading words that are on glossy white paper.

____ ____ 70. When reading, words or letters shift, shake, blur, move, run together, disappear, or become difficult to perceive.

____ ____ 71. I feel tense, tired, or sleepy or even get headaches when reading.

____ ____ 72. I have problems judging distance and have difficulty with such things as escalators, stairs, ball sports, or driving.

Sensory Integration Issues

____ ____ 73. I seem to be more sensitive to the environment than others.

____ ____ 74. I am more sensitive to noise than others.

____ ____ 75. I am particularly sensitive to touch or certain clothing or tags.

____ ____ 76. I have unusual sensitivity to certain smells.

____ ____ 77. I have unusual sensitivity to light.

____ ____ 78. I am sensitive to movement or crave spinning activities.

____ ____ 79. I tend to be clumsy or accident-prone.

Inattention

___ ___ 80. I fail to give close attention to details or make careless mistakes.

___ ___ 81. I have trouble sustaining attention in routine situations, such as homework, chores, or paperwork.

___ ___ 82. I have trouble listening.

___ ___ 83. I fail to finish things.

___ ___ 84. I have poor organization for time or space, such as backpack, room, desk, or paperwork.

___ ___ 85. I avoid, dislike, or am reluctant to engage in tasks that require sustained mental effort.

___ ___ 86. I lose things.

___ ___ 87. I am easily distracted.

___ ___ 88. I am forgetful.

Hyperactivity/Impulsivity

___ ___ 89. I am fidgety or restless or have trouble sitting still.

___ ___ 90. I have difficulty remaining seated in situations where remaining seated is expected.

___ ___ 91. I run about or climb excessively in situations in which it is inappropriate.

___ ___ 92. I have difficulty playing quietly.

___ ___ 93. I am always "on the go" or act as if "driven by a motor."

___ ___ 94. I talk excessively.

___ ___ 95. I blurt out answers before questions have been completed.

___ ___ 96. I have difficulty awaiting my turn.

___ ___ 97. I interrupt or intrude on others (e.g., butt into conversations or games).

___ ___ 98. I am impulsive, saying or doing things without thinking first.

AMEN CLINIC LEARNING DISABILITY SCREENING QUESTIONNAIRE KEY

Questions 1–79:

More than 2 answers in each section with a score of 3 or 4 should be investigated. Consider seeing a learning specialist or school psychologist for further testing.

Questions 80–98:

Attention deficit hyperactivity disorder (ADHD), combined type if both 80–88 and 89–98 score as follows:

Highly probable	6 questions with a score of 3 or 4
Probable	5 questions with a score of 3 or 4
May be possible	3 questions with a score of 3 or 4

Attention deficit disorder (ADD), inattentive subtype if 80–88 has more than 5 questions with 3 or 4 but 89–98 has less than 2 questions with a score of 3 or 4:

Highly probable	6 questions with a score of 3 or 4
Probable	5 questions with a score of 3 or 4
May be possible	3 questions with a score of 3 or 4

RESOURCES

Amen Clinics
www.amenclinics.com

Amen Clinics, Inc. (ACI), was established in 1989 by Daniel G. Amen, MD. We specialize in innovative diagnosis and treatment planning for a wide variety of behavioral, learning, emotional, cognitive, and weight issues for children, teenagers, and adults. ACI has an international reputation for evaluating brain-behavior problems, such as ADD/ADHD, depression, anxiety, school failure, traumatic brain injury and concussion, obsessive-compulsive disorders, aggressiveness, marital conflict, cognitive decline, brain toxicity from drugs or alcohol, and obesity. In addition, we work with people to optimize brain function and decrease the risk for Alzheimer's disease and other age-related issues.

Brain SPECT imaging is performed in the clinics. ACI has the world's largest database of brain scans for emotional, cognitive, and behavioral problems. ACI welcomes referrals from physicians, psychologists, social workers, marriage and family therapists, drug and alcohol counselors, and individual patients and families.

Our toll-free number is (888) 912-7813.

Amen Clinics Orange County,
California
3150 Bristol Street, Suite 400
Costa Mesa, CA 92626

Amen Clinics Northern
California
350 North Wiget Lane, Suite 105
Walnut Creek, CA 94598

Amen Clinics Northwest
616 120th Avenue NE, Suite C100
Bellevue, WA 98005

Amen Clinics Los Angeles
5363 Balboa Boulevard, Suite 100
Encino, CA 91316

Amen Clinics Washington, DC
10701 Parkridge Boulevard,
Suite 110
Reston, VA 20191

Amen Clinics New York
16 East 40th Street, 9th Floor
New York, NY 10016

Amen Clinics Atlanta
5901 Peachtree Dunwoody Road,
NE, Suite C65
Atlanta, GA 30328

Amen Clinics Chicago
2333 Waukegan Road, Suite 150
Bannockburn, Il 60015

Amen Clinics Dallas
Coming soon

Brain Fit Life
www.mybrainfitlife.com

Based on Dr. Amen's 35 years as a clinical psychiatrist, he and his wife, Tana, have developed a sophisticated online community to help you feel smarter, happier, and younger. It includes:

- Detailed questionnaires to help you know your brain type and a personalized program targeted to your own needs
- WebNeuro, a sophisticated neuropsychological test that assesses your brain
- Fun brain games and tools to boost your motivation
- Exclusive, award-winning, 24/7 brain gym membership
- Physical exercises and tutorials led by Tana
- Hundreds of Tana's delicious, brain-healthy recipes
- Exercises to kill the ANTs (automatic negative thoughts)
- Meditation and hypnosis audios for sleep, anxiety, overcoming weight issues, pain, and peak performance
- Amazing brain-enhancing music from Grammy Award winner Barry Goldstein

- Online forum for questions and answers and a community of support
- Access to monthly live coaching calls with Daniel and Tana

BrainMD Health
www.brainmdhealth.com

BrainMD Health offers the highest-quality brain health supplements, as well as courses, books, and information products on optimizing brain health. Among the courses offered is one that teaches high school and college students how to love and care for their brains. Called Brain Thrive by 25 (www.brainthriveby25.com), it has been taught in all 50 states and seven countries. Independent research has shown that it reduces drug, alcohol, and tobacco use; decreases depression; and improves self-esteem. In the course, we teach students to love and care for their brains, including lessons on basic brain facts, the developing brain, gender differences, the impact of drugs and alcohol on the brain, nutrition, stress management, killing ANTs (automatic negative thoughts), and how to throw a brain healthy party. It has been a popular course that has changed lives of those who take it.

REFERENCES

Introduction

1. Kaufman SB. Learning strategies outperform IQ in predicting achievement. *Scientific American*, April 8, 2013. https://blogs. scientificamerican.com/beautiful-minds/learning-strategies-outperform-iq-in-predicting-achievement/.

Chapter 4

1. Ophir E, Nass C, and Wagner AD. Cognitive control in media multitaskers. PNAS. 2009;106(37):15583-15587. https://doi. org/10.1073/pnas.0903620106.
2. Hubbert B. How room temperature affects your brain while studying. Champion AC. 2017. Dec. https://www.championac.com/ blog/how-room-temperature-affects-your-brain-while-studying/.
3. Chang A-M, Aeschbach D, Duffy JF, et al. Evening use of light-emitting eReaders negatively affects sleep, circadian timing, next-morning alertness. PNAS. 2015;112(4):1232–1237.
4. Ariga A and Lleras A. Brief and rare mental "breaks" keep you focused: deactivation and reactivation of task goals preempt vigilance decrements. *Cognition*. 2011 Mar;118(3):439–443.

Chapter 5

1. Felger JC, Li Z, Haroon E, et al. Inflammation is associated with decreased functional connectivity within corticostriatal reward circuitry in depression. Mol Psychiatry. 2016;21:1358–1365.
2. Ford, G. Inflammation in psychiatric disorders. *European Psychiatry*, 2014 Nov;29(8S):551–552.

3. Miller AH, Haroon E, and Felger JC. Therapeutic implications of brain-immune interactions: treatment in translation. *Neuropsychopharmacol.* 2017;42:334–359.
4. Lajiness-O'Neill R, Erdodi L, and Bigler ED. Memory and learning in pediatric traumatic brain injury: a review and examination of moderators of outcome. *Appl Neuropsychol.* 2010 Apr;17(2):83–92.
5. Schachar RJ, Park LS, and Dennis M. Mental health implications of traumatic brain injury (TBI) in children and youth. J Can Acad Child Adolesc Psychiatry. 2015 Fall;24(2):100–108.
6. Zaninotto AL, Vicentini JE, Fregni F, et al. Updates and current perspectives of psychiatric assessments after traumatic brain injury: a systematic review. *Front Psychiatry.* 2016 Jun 14;7:95.
7. Schachar, et al.
8. Mackelprang JL, Harpin SB, Grubenhoff JA, et al. Adverse outcomes among homeless adolescents and young adults who report a history of traumatic brain injury. *Am J Public Health.* 2014 Oct;104(10):1986–1992.

Chapter 6

1. Peck SM. *The Road Less Traveled.* New York: Touchstone, 2003.

Chapter 8

1. Hölzel BK, Carmody J, Vangel M, et al. Mindfulness practice leads to increases in regional brain gray matter density. Psychiatry Res. 2010;191(1):36-43. doi: 10.1016/j.pscychresns.2010.08.006.
2. Glass A and Kang M. Dividing attention in the classroom reduces exam performance. *Educational Psychology.* 2018. https://www.tandfonline.com/doi/full/10.1080/01443410.2018.1489046.

Chapter 12

1. Weyandt LL, White TL, Gudmundsdottir BG, et al. Neurocognitive, autonomic, and mood effects of Adderall: a pilot study of healthy

college students. *Pharmacy* 6(3). https://www.mdpi.com/2226–4787/6/3/58.

2. Taren AA, Gianaros PJ, Greco CM, et al. Mindfulness meditation training and executive control Network resting state functional connectivity: a randomized controlled trial. *Psychosom Med.* 2017;79(6):674–683.

3. Tang YJ, Yang L, Leve LD, et al. Improving executive function and its neurobiological mechanisms through a mindfulness-based intervention: advances within the field of developmental neuroscience. *Child Dev Perspect.* 2012 Dec; 6(4):361–366.

4. Maller C, Townsend M, Pryor A, et al. Healthy nature healthy people: "contact with nature" as an upstream health promotion intervention for populations. *Health Promot Int.* 2006 Mar;21(1):45–54.

5. Lambrou P. Fun with fractals? *Psychology Today.* 2012. Sep. https://www.psychologytoday.com/blog/codes-joy/201209/fun-fractals.

6. Kasper S, Gastpar M, Müller WE, et al. Lavender oil preparation Silexan is effective in generalized anxiety disorder: a randomized, double-blind comparison to placebo and paroxetine. *Int J Neuropsychopharmacol.* 2014 Jun;17(6):859–869.

7. Koulivand PH, Khaleghi Ghadiri M, and Gorji A. Lavender and the nervous system: evidence-based complementary and alternative medicine. *eCAM.* 2013. 681304.

8. Kheirkhah M, Vali Pour NS, Nisani L, et al. Comparing the effects of aromatherapy with rose oils and warm foot bath on anxiety in the first stage of labor in nulliparous women. *Iran Red Crescent Med J.* 2014 Aug 17;16(9):e14455.

9. Hongratanaworakit T. Relaxing effect of rose oil on humans. Nat Prod Commun. 2009 Feb;4(2):291–296.

10. Amsterdam JD, Shults J, Soeller I, et al. Chamomile (Matricaria recutita) may provide antidepressant activity in anxious, depressed humans: an exploratory study. *Altern Ther Health Med.* 2012 Sep-Oct;18(5):44–49.

11. Herbs and spices. *All Women's Talk.* http://health.allwomenstalk.com/ways-to-improve-your-mood-with-food/4.

Chapter 14

1. Carretié L, Mercado F, Tapia M, et al. Emotion, attention, and the 'negativity bias', studied through event-related potentials. *International Journal of Psychophysiology*. 2001;41(1):75-85. https://www.ncbi.nlm.nih.gov/pubmed/11239699.
2. https://www.outbrain.com/blog/headlines-when-the-best-brings -the-worst-and-the-worst-brings-the-best/?utm_source=Silverpop Mailing&utm_medium=email&utm_campaign=BrainpowerWeekly -2014-2February19(Non-LT)%2520(1)&utm_content=.

Appendix A

1. High blood pressure during childhood and adolescence. Centers for Disease Control and Prevention. 2018. July. https://www.cdc.gov/bloodpressure/youth.htm.
2. Berk LS et al. Modulation of neuroimmune parameters during the eustress of humor-associated mirthful laughter. *Altern Ther Health Med*. 2001 Mar;7(2):62-72, 74-6.
3. Ryu KH et al. Effects of Laughter Therapy on Immune Responses in Postpartum Women. *J Altern Complement Med*. 2015 Dec;21(12):781-8.
4. Cousins N. Anatomy of an illness (as perceived by the patient). *N Engl J Med*. 1976 Dec 23;295(26):1458-63.

ABOUT DANIEL G. AMEN, MD

The *Washington Post* has called Dr. Amen the most popular psychiatrist in America, and Sharecare named him the web's #1 most influential expert and advocate on mental health.

Dr. Amen is a physician, board-certified child, adolescent, and adult psychiatrist, 10-time *New York Times* bestselling author, and international speaker. He is the founder of Amen Clinics in Costa Mesa, Encino, and San Francisco, California; Bellevue, Washington; Reston, Virginia; Atlanta, Georgia; New York, New York; and Chicago, Illinois. Amen Clinics have one of the highest published success rates in treating complex psychiatric issues, and they have built the world's largest database of functional brain scans, totaling nearly 170,000 scans on patients from 120 countries.

Dr. Amen is the lead researcher on the world's largest brain imaging and rehabilitation study on professional football players. His research has not only demonstrated high levels of brain damage in players, it also showed the possibility of significant recovery for many with the principles that underlie his work.

Together with Pastor Rick Warren and Mark Hyman, MD, Dr. Amen is one of the chief architects of Saddleback Church's "Daniel Plan," a program to get the world healthy through religious organizations.

Dr. Amen is the author or co-author of more than 70 professional articles, seven book chapters, and more than 30 books, including the #1 *New York Times* bestsellers *The Daniel Plan* and *Change Your Brain, Change Your Life,* as well as *Magnificent Mind at Any Age, Change Your Brain, Change Your Body, Use Your Brain to Change Your Age, Healing ADD, The Brain Warrior's Way, The Brain Warrior's Way Cookbook, Memory Rescue,* and *Feel Better Fast and Make It Last.*

Dr. Amen's published scientific articles have appeared in the prestigious journals *Brain Imaging and Behavior, Molecular Psychiatry, PLOS One, Translational Psychiatry, International Journal of Obesity, Journal of Neuropsychiatry and Clinical Neurosciences, Minerva Psichiatrica, Journal of Neurotrauma, American Journal of Psychiatry, Nuclear Medicine Communications, Neurological Research, Journal of the American Academy of Child and Adolescent Psychiatry, Primary Psychiatry, Military Medicine,* and *General Hospital Psychiatry.* His research on posttraumatic stress disorder and traumatic brain injury was recognized by *Discover* magazine in its Year in Science issue as one of the "100 Top Stories of 2015."

Dr. Amen has written, produced, and hosted 13 popular shows about the brain on public television. He has appeared in documentary films including *After the Last Round* and *The Crash Reel,* and on Emmy-winning television shows such as *The Truth about Drinking* and the *Dr. Oz Show.* He was a consultant on the movie *Concussion,* starring Will Smith. He has also spoken for the National Security Agency (NSA), the National Science Foundation (NSF), Harvard University's Learning and the Brain Conference, the US Department of the Interior, the National Council of Juvenile and Family Court Judges, and the Supreme Courts of Delaware, Ohio, and Wyoming. Dr. Amen's work has been featured in *Newsweek, Time* magazine, *Huffington Post, BBC, The Guardian, Parade* magazine, *New York Times, New York Times Magazine, Washington Post, LA Times, Men's Health,* and *Cosmopolitan.*

Dr. Amen is married to Tana, the father of four children, and grandfather to Elias, Emmy, Liam, Louie, and Haven. He is an avid table tennis player.

ABOUT CHLOE AMEN

Chloe Amen is a sophomore in high school. She is a member of the National Honor Society, a guest star on the popular public television show *Feel Better Fast,* and a contributor and guest star in the high school program *Brain Thrive by 25,* designed to help teens improve brain function and performance. She is an intern for the Mayor's Youth Council of Newport Beach, California, which participates in local government and community service. Chloe also has a passion for service and is an active volunteer for Girls Inc., an after-school girls' empowerment program. Volunteering at church in activities such as student leadership and campus cleanup has been an ongoing devotion. In her free time, Chloe enjoys practicing martial arts, dance, songwriting and singing, and the arts. In elementary and early junior high, Chloe struggled with anxiety and organization, which affected her academic performance. Through the techniques she has learned and shared in this book, she has transformed her mindset and work ethic. As a result, she now has a 4.0 GPA and enjoys her education.

ABOUT ALIZÉ CASTELLANOS

Alizé Castellanos is a ninth grader in Orange County, California. She is an Honor Society student and participates in cross country and track and field. In the last year, she has been awarded Language Arts Student of the Year, Life Science Student of the Year, Automation and Robotics Student of the Year, and Student of the Semester on three different occasions. In addition, she was voted class clown by her peers, because she also spends time having fun. Alizé was recently diagnosed with ADHD and works very hard to maintain good grades using the skills in this book. She especially loves learning how to kill the ANTs (automatic negative thoughts) that try to mess up her life.

GRATITUDE AND APPRECIATION

So many people have been involved in the process of creating *Change Your Brain, Change Your Grades*. I am grateful to them all, especially the tens of thousands of patients and families who have come to Amen Clinics and allowed us to help them on their healing journey.

I am grateful to the amazing staff at Amen Clinics, who work hard every day serving our patients. Special appreciation to Frances Sharpe, Chloe Amen, and Alizé Castellanos, who helped me craft the book to make it easily accessible to our readers. I hope you agree.

Of course, I am grateful to my amazing wife, Tana, who is my partner in all I do, and to my family, who have tolerated my obsession with making brains better, especially my other children, Antony, Breanne, and Kaitlyn; grandchildren; and parents, Louis and Dorie Amen.